Terrorism: Creating a Climate of Fear

SAGHIR IQBAL

ISBN-10: 1724714856
ISBN-13: 978-1724714855

DEDICATION

I dedicate this book to all those who gave me encouragement, support and guidance. Foremost, to my father (late) Raja Mohammed Iqbal and to my mother Azra Begum, from whom I have learnt so much.

CONTENTS

ACKNOWLEDGMENTS

I am very grateful to a host of people for their various contributions towards this book. I am particularly very grateful to Professor Syed Peerzada Mahmud Shah Bookhari who deserves much commendation for his constant encouragement and support throughout the hard times of the programme.

SAGHIR IQBAL

Terrorism: Creating a Climate of Fear

Motivations for Present Day Terrorism

Abstract

This book looks at the concept of terrorism and the techniques that are available to different kinds of groups pursuing different types of objectives. However it is difficult to define terrorism because all acts of terrorism are open to interpretation. This is primarily the main reason why the term has not been universally accepted by all scholars or academics.

There are many reasons why political groups attempt to bring about radical change through terrorism. People are often frustrated with their position in society. They may in some way feel persecuted or oppressed because of their race, religion, or they feel exploited by a government. Any group that uses terrorist actions have very complex and powerful reasons to engage in those activities.

The usual experience of violence by a stronger party has historically turned victims into terrorists. State terror very often breeds collective terror. Because 'terrorism' is a word that has been used so much and so loosely that it has lost a clear meaning.

Anti-terrorist police operations

Abbreviation

ALCM/GLCM – Air Launched Cruise Missile/ Ground Launched Cruise Missile

BLA – Baluchistan Liberation Army

CIA – Central Intelligence Agency

FATA – Federally Administered Tribal Areas

HRW - Human Rights Watch

ISR - Intelligence, Surveillance and reconnaissance

ISAF -   International Security Assistance Force

IRA - Irish Republican Army

LGB - Laser guided bombs

MIC – Military-Industrial Complex

NIC - US National Intelligence Council

NATO - North Atlantic Treaty Organisation

PAF – Pakistan Air Force

PGM - Precision guided munitions (Smart weapons)

PLO – Palestine Liberation Organisation

RAW – Research and Analysis Wing

UAV – Unmanned Aerial Vehicle

UCAV – Unmanned Combat Aerial Vehicle

UK - United Kingdom

UN - United Nations

UNSC - United Nations Security Council

USA - United States of America

WMD - Weapons of Mass Destruction

ZANU – Zimbabwe African National Union

After a recent terror attack many European leaders criticized social media to do more to fight terrorism, Facebook said its using AI to combat terrorism.

1 TERRORISM: DEFINITION

Terrorism

The definitions of a terrorist or terrorism is one that is quite difficult to define. Even though most people can recognise terrorism when they see it, the leading experts still have difficulties agreeing on one definition. As a result numerous different definitions have come about from varying different governmental and non-governmental organisations.

Terrorism is a technique that is available to different kinds of groups pursuing different types of objectives. It is the unlawful or threatened use of force or violence on people or property to compel or intimidate governments or societies, often to achieve political, religious, or ideological objectives. However it is difficult to define terrorism because all acts of terrorism are open to interpretation.[1] This is primarily the main reason why the term has not been universally accepted by all scholars or academics.

The reason for the definitional and theoretical disagreements are primarily due to the lack of agreement over what covers terrorist activities and related phenomena such as guerrilla groups or violent protest movements; and the

---

[1] Alan Collins, Contemporary Security Studies, Oxford University Press, 2007, p303.

difficulty of making a distinction between activities related to 'legitimate' acts of national self-determination struggles and 'illegal' acts of violence against governments.

Firearms instructors play the role of terrorists during a Metropolitan Police training programme for armed officers in the UK

It is usually argued that what may constitute genuine struggles for national self-determination may be labelled terrorism by those that might not approve of the activities of the group. The term 'terrorism' is routinely applied to non-state political violence but this is as expected unhelpful since states frequently terrorize their own and other state's citizens.[2]

We will look at some of the definitions given on terrorism; a brief historical account of terrorism; state the various types of terrorism and their reasons and then account for the difficulty in achieving a universally accepted definition.

Definitions

In 1983 Alex Schmid listed 109 definitions on terrorism.[3] We will look at the following two definitions; according to Martha Crenshaw,

---

[2] Peter Hough, Understanding Global Security, Routledge, 2004, p81.

[3] Adrian Guelke, The Age of Terrorism and the International Political System, I.B Tauris Publishers & Co Ltd, 1998, p19.

"Terrorism is the deliberate and systematic use or threat of violence to coerce change in political behaviour. It involves symbolic acts of violence, intended to communicate a political message to watching audiences".[4]

The American Central Intelligence Agency (CIA) defines terrorism as the following:

Terrorism: The threat or use of violence for political purposes by individuals or groups, whether acting for or in opposition to established governmental authority, when such actions are intended to shock, stun, or intimidate a target group wider than the immediate victims. Terrorism has involved groups seeking to overthrow specific regimes, to rectify perceived national or group grievances, or to undermine international order as an end in itself. [5]

The above definition has also been accepted by the US State department. However, the above definition had led to many misunderstanding on the nature of terrorism. For example, this formula would include the French resistance in Nazi-occupied France during World War II, the IRA in Northern Ireland, the Basques in Spain, Ku Klux Klan in the US; Mao's Cultural Revolution in China, Stalin's purges in the Soviet Union and the Contras in Nicaragua. (6)[6]

This tendency to group all forms of unconventional warfare under the umbrella of terrorism enables us to attach a 'terrorist' label to every act of violence, a label that is often of considerable propaganda value to the opposing governments. For example, the Afghan Mujahedeen (once labelled as 'freedom fighters' when fighting the former Soviet Union's occupation of their country) in Afghanistan are classed as terrorists along with the Red Brigade in Italy even though they are different forces with

---

[4] Conteh-Morgan, Collective Political Violence – An Introduction to the Theories and Cases of Violent Conflicts, Routledge, 2004, p255.

[5] James Adams, The Financing of Terror, New English Library, 1988, p7.

[6] Ibid

different aims and methods of operations.[7]

In addition, states that oppose terrorism and do so in the name of an existing society may themselves commit acts of terrorism. The Allied bombings of Germany in World War II was a form of terrorism in that it was designed to intimidate civilians, and some of the actions of the US army in Vietnam, such as the My Lai massacre, could be classed as 'terrorist'.[8]

IRA

The definition of terrorism should not be restricted by political or national barriers. However, for the US and British governments, and many others, the word 'terrorist' has come to mean any form of violent activity with which a particular government happens to disagree. Terrorism has thus become a propaganda tool. For example, the British refer to the IRA as terrorist but to the PLO as guerrillas, a distinction that has always infuriated the Israelis who see no difference. (9)[9]

---

[7] Op cit:8

[8] Frank Barnaby, Instruments of Terror, Vision Paperbacks, 1996, p45.

[9] Ibid

Former PLO leader – Yasser Arafat

Furthermore, across the globe we can see how those initially labelled as terrorists change into 'freedom fighters' and then democratic leaders, for example, the former leader of South Africa - Nelson Mandela. Another example, is that of the 'Taleban' in Afghanistan, they were previously known by the Western powers as the Mujahedeen (freedom fighters) when fighting the Soviets troops but now as 'terrorists'. The Taleban see themselves as freedom fighter's trying to eradicate foreign troops from their country.[10]

---

[10] Terrorism (Internet): www. http://en.wikipedia.org/wiki/Terrorism

Mandela taken off US terror list

US President George W Bush has signed a bill removing Nelson Mandela and South African leaders from the US terror watch list, officials say.

Mr Mandela and ANC party members will now be able to visit the US without a waiver from the secretary of state.

The African National Congress (ANC) was designated as a terrorist organisation by South Africa's old apartheid regime.

A US senator said the new legislation was a step towards removing the "shame of dishonouring this great leader".

'Rather embarrassing'

Nelson Mandela was South Africa's first post-apartheid-era president

http://superforestnyc.blogspot.com/2008/07/mandela-taken-off-us-terror-list.html

Mujahedeen freedom fighters (USA's designation) when fighting with the Russians in Afghanistan

In the 1980s the Mujahedeen were known as freedom fighters – the Irony is the same group later became know as the Taliban terrorists after they did not serve US or its allies interests.

Terrorists or "Freedom Fighters"? [11]

Afghan Mujahedeen/Taliban

---

[11] Terrorists or "Freedom Fighters"? Recruited by the CIA -
http://www.globalresearch.ca/terrorists-or-freedom-fighters-recruited-by-the-cia/5429766

Who is a terrorist?

- States reserve for themselves the power to define who is a terrorist
- In the 1980s, the USA regarded the Afghan Mujahideen as 'freedom fighters' when they resisted the Soviet invasion
- Two decades later, the USA accused a new generation of Afghans of being terrorists for resisting western invasion

The above images, show the various depictions of terrorism and freedom fighters when it suits the needs of powerful states. To punish the Russians and give them a 'taste of Vietnam, a conflict in which the Americans suffered huge military and economic losses by the Vietcong who were supported by the Russians'. The US labelled the rebel groups fighting the Russians as freedom fighters (Mujahideen). The Mujahedeen were the freedom fighters in the eyes of the West

When the Russians were defeated in Afghanistan, - aka the 'Taliban' became the terrorist as they were against western interests or interventions in the region. However, the irony is that the Russians are supporting the Taliban against US and its allies interests. The US accuses Russia of trying to undermine Afghanistan by supporting the Taliban.[12]

---

[12] Is Russia arming the Afghan Taliban? https://www.bbc.co.uk/news/world-asia-41842285

2 CREATING A CLIMATE OF FEAR

Australian Counter Terrorism Response Group

Terrorism ultimately involves the use or threat of violence with the aim of creating fear not only to the victims but among a wider audience; it is fear which distinguishes terrorism from both conventional and guerrilla warfare. While both conventional military forces may engage in psychological warfare and guerrilla forces may engage in acts of terror and other forms of propaganda, they both aim at military victory.

Terrorism on the other hand aims to achieve political or other goals, when direct military victory is not possible. This has resulted in some social scientists referring to guerrilla warfare as the 'weapon of the weak' and terrorism as the 'weapon of the weakest'.[13]

Background

Historically, the use of terror to achieve goals is not a new idea. One early terrorist group, the assassins, thrived in the 12th centuries. The assassins used murder to dispose of their enemies, and their name has come to be used for one who kills for political or religious reasons. Government terrorism dates at least from immediately after the French Revolution, in 1789. During this period, known as the 'Reign of Terror', the French Revolutionary executed thousands of its citizens who were considered

---

13 Ibid

enemies of its rule.[14]

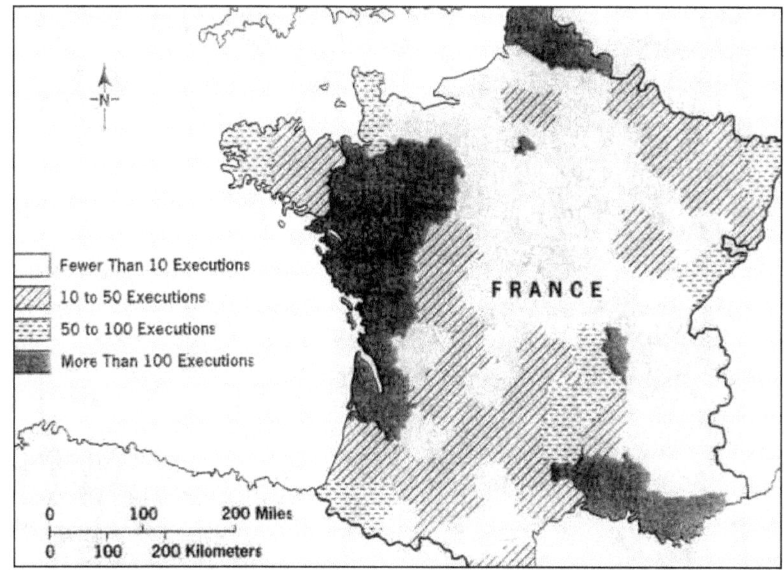

http://www.maherpages.net/mrmaher/apeuro/apeuro_unit_4/reign_of_terror.htm

https://www.slideshare.net/tomrichey/the-reign-of-terror-french-revolution-17931794

---

[14] Lawrence Freedman, Superterrorism Policy Responses, Blackwell Publishing Ltd, 2002, p14.

Acts of terrorism have been committed by individuals, or groups who seek national independence. One such act was the assassination of the Arch Duke Ferdinanz of France in 1914. The assassination had sought to win Bosnia from Austrian rule, but failed and led to the outbreak of World War I.[15]

Franz Ferdinand

Monarchs and government officials are often the targets of terrorism. In Russia (1881), members of a terrorist group that wanted to overthrow the government assassinated Czar Alexander. Politically unstable countries offer frequent opportunities for terrorism. Lebanon, which has been torn by years of Civil War and instability , has been the sight of numerous terrorist attacks.[16]

In addition to terrorist groups, governments have also engaged in terrorism. Countries sometimes use terrorism (State-sponsored terrorism) as a substitute for traditional warfare by providing money, training, and weapons to terrorist groups whose activities serve their national aims.

Governments may also plan and carry out terrorist actions themselves, although they usually deny responsibility for them.[17] The US bombings of targets in Libya (Tripoli and Benghazi) in 1986 were justified by American and British Governments, despite many civilians being killed. [18]

---

[15] Ibid

[16] op cit:15

[17] Lawrence Freedman, Christopher Hill, Adam Roberts, R.J. Vincent, Paul Wilkinson and Philip Windsor, Terrorism and International Order, Routledge & Keegan Paul Ltd, 1986, p20.

[18] Ibid

http://remembertheintrepid.blogspot.com/2008/09/operation-el-dorado-canyon.html

Operation El Dorado Canyon and Bombing Libya in 1986[19]

---

[19] https://www.thoughtco.com/international-terrorism-bombing-libya-operation-2360529

On 14 April 1986, twenty four F-111Fs strike combat aircraft of the USAF 48th Tactical Fighter Wing took off from the Royal Air Force base at Lakenheath, United Kingdom.[20]

---

[20] http://eightiesclub.tripod.com/id313.htm

US F-111 conducting an airstrike against Tripoli, Libya in 1986

The US bombings of targets in Libya in 1986 were justified by American and British Governments, despite many civilians being killed – some have labelled this as nothing more than 'state terrorism'.

We will now look briefly at the various forms of terrorism in order to understand some of the reasons for not being able to find a universally accepted definition.

3 WAR TERRORISM

Terror suspect arrested in Greece

War terrorism is violence used indiscriminately against a civilian or non-military population, the motive of the people who use this type of terrorism is to win a war. An example of this is, is the first dropping of the atomic bomb on Hiroshima and Nagasaki at the end of World War II. This killed 70-100,000 people immediately and a possible 200,000 dead from radiation sickness within the next five years.

The argument for this was to end the war, to avoid the potentially massive allied losses that an invasion would cost. The victims for this were civilians and not military so this could be interpreted as an act of terrorism even if it was justified by the government as a necessity of war.[21]

---

[21] Hiroshima (Internet Website - Wikipedia, the free encyclopedia) http://en.wikipedia.org/wiki/Hiroshima

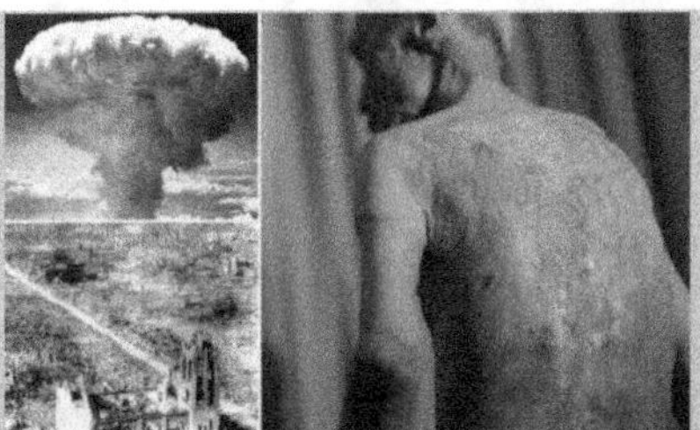

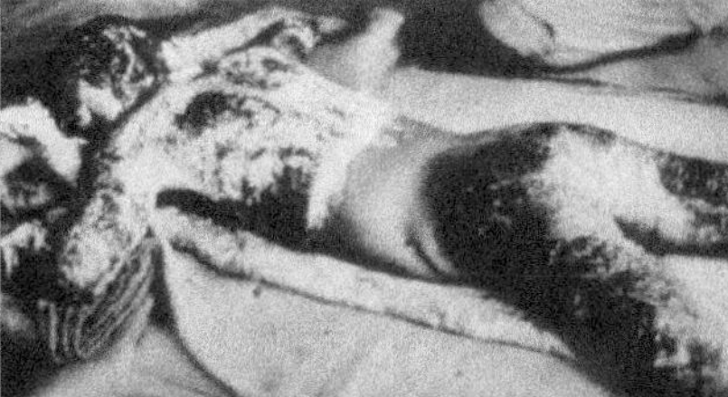

Horrific injuries due to a nuclear bomb (Hiroshima and Nagasaki - Japan)

Horrific injuries caused by a nuclear bomb

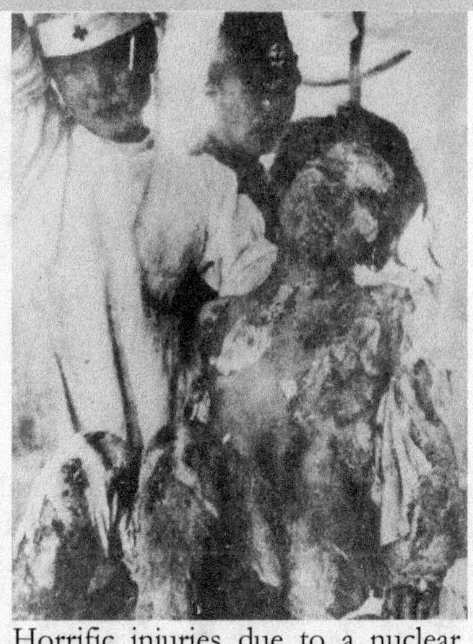

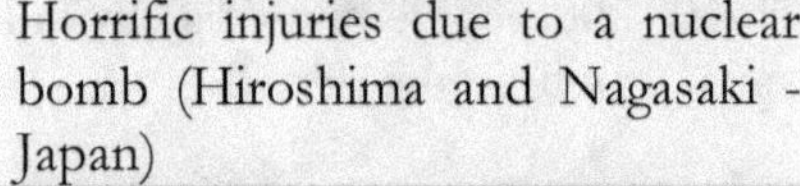

Horrific injuries due to a nuclear bomb (Hiroshima and Nagasaki - Japan)

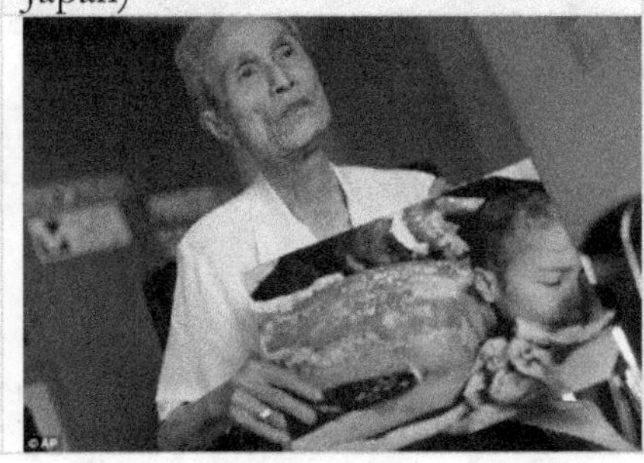

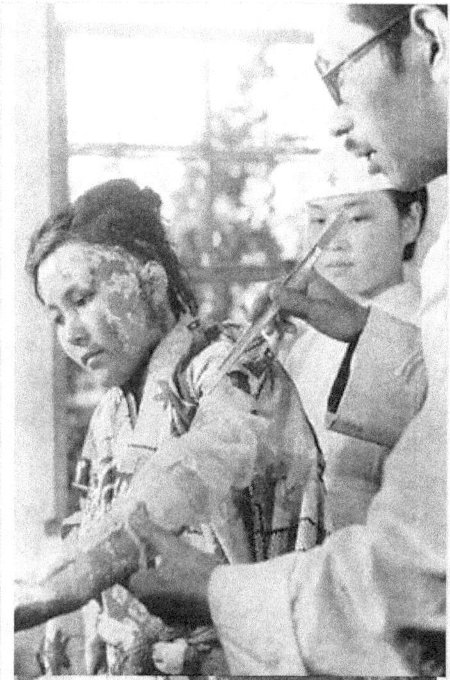

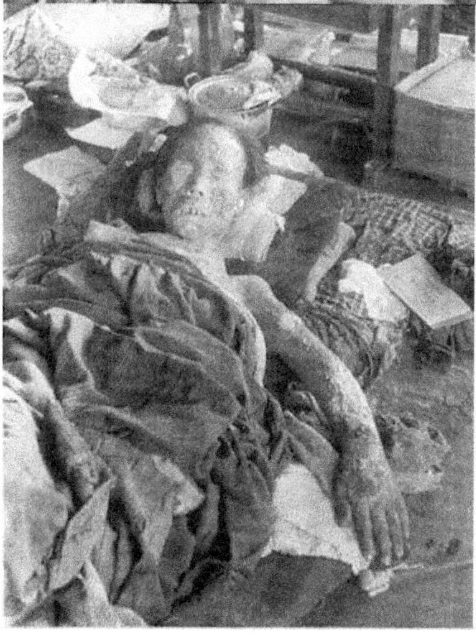

Nuclear devastation caused by the nuclear bombs dropped by the USA on Japan - Hiroshima and Nagasaki cities were destroyed with horrendous injuries and casualties.

The devastations on the civilian populations of Hiroshima and Nagasaki was to some a terrorist act.

Vietnam war

The Vietnam War was a devastating war in which more than 3 million people, including 58,000 Americans, were killed in the conflict.[22] The conflict was between the North Vietnam and its southern allies the Viet Cong and South Vietnam with United States as its major ally. The war was lost by South Vietnam and resulted in US withdrawal in 1973 – thereby ensuring the unification of Vietnam under the North's control (communist government). The war was also part of a larger regional conflict and of the Cold War between the United States and the Soviet Union and their respective allies.[23]

US Soldiers in Vietnam

---

[22] https://www.history.com/topics/vietnam-war

[23] https://www.britannica.com/event/Vietnam-War

American airpower caused considerable damage to Vietnam and killed many people

'Carpet' bombing vietnam

US B-52 Bombers dropping their destructive payload on Vietnam

Aftermath of Vietnam Saigon bombing

Rwanda genocide

In April-July 1994 the world was shocked by the genocide committed by Rwanda's Hutu Majority population against its minority Tutsis. The genocide was planned by extremist individuals of Rwanda's majority Hutu population. The plan was to exterminate the minority Tutsi population and anyone who opposed those genocidal intentions. In approximately 3 months, an estimated 200,000 Hutu, encouraged on by propaganda from various media outlets, participated in the genocide. More than 800,000 civilians (primarily Tutsi, but also moderate Hutu) were killed during the campaign. As many as 2,000,000 Rwandans fled the country during or immediately after the genocide.[24]

Rwandan armed forces had killed 10 Belgian peacekeeping officers, in a successful effort to dissuade international intervention in the genocide that had begun only hours earlier. The French were allies of the Hutu government and had sent a force to set up a supposedly safe zone but were

---

[24] https://www.britannica.com/event/Rwanda-genocide-of-1994

accused by many of not doing enough to stop the mass killings in that area. Rwanda's current president had blamed France of taking part in the massacres - a charge vehemently denied by the French.

French forces in Rwanda were accused of not doing enough to stop the killing[25]

Thousands of innocent people were hacked to death with machetes by their neighbours

---

[25] https://www.bbc.co.uk/news/world-africa-26875506

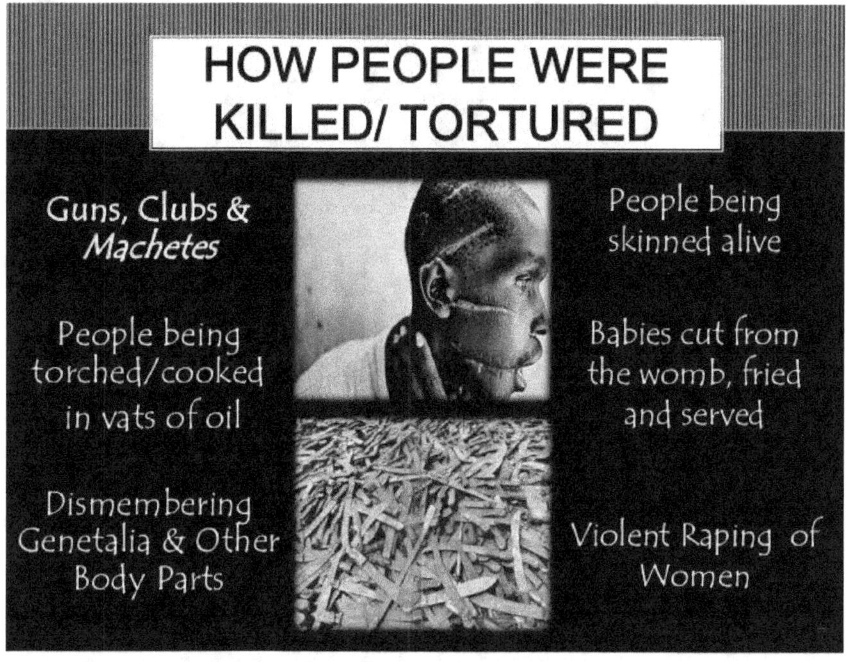

Rwandan radio stations were broadcasting instructions to the Hutu majority to kill all minority Tutsis in the country. It was said that, the army and the national police were directing the mass slaughter and murder, sometimes threatening Hutu civilians when encouragement didn't work. Many hundreds of thousands of innocent people were hacked to death with machetes by their neighbours.[26]

It was unbelievable that this scale of killing and murder could take place in a very short duration. It was a great shame that the international community could not muster a force to put a stop to this madness and apprehend the inciters and killers of this genocide.

---

[26] https://www.bbc.co.uk/news/world-africa-26875506

Many people were massacred

Chechnya

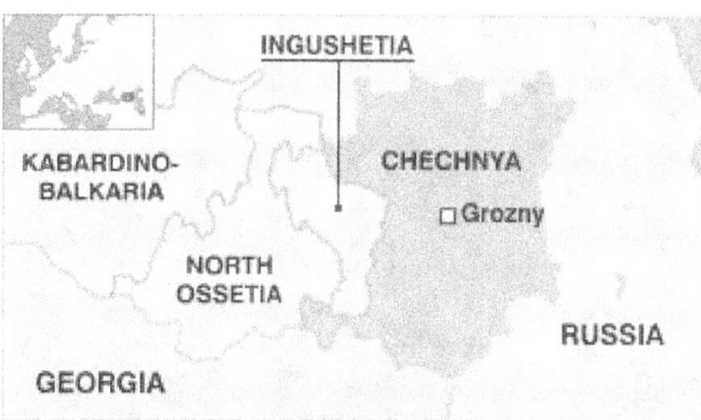

Chechnya has had tense relations with the Russian federation and had desired independence from them. In December 1994, Russian troops entered Chechnya, in order to prevent Chechnya's effort to secede from the Russian Federation. This resulted in intense battle between Russian soldiers and Chechnya's rebels that were seeking an independent country. It was estimated that tens of thousands of civilians were killed and over 500,000 persons displaced since the conflict began.[27]

The Russian aim was for a quick victory leading to pacification and reestablishment of a pro-Russian government in Chechnya. However, there was fierce resistance from Chechnya's separatists who had inflicted serious losses on Russian military forces. [28]

The capital Grozny was flattened in 1994 by the Russian army in its conflict with Chechnya's separatist movement

---

[27] https://www.bbc.com/news/world-europe-18188085

[28] https://www.globalsecurity.org/military/world/war/chechnya1.htm

Chechen volunteers gather in the capital in 1994 in the hope of protecting it from the Russian army[29]

The atrocities committed by Russian forces in Chechnya were well noted: In Grozny, the graffiti on the walls reads **"Welcome to Hell: Part Two,"** about as good a summary as any of what Chechen civilians have been living through in the past few months. There is widespread evidence that indicates that Russian forces have committed serious abuses, including war crimes in Chechnya. [30]

Russian troops in action

---

[29] https://www.bbc.com/news/world-europe-18188085

[30] https://www.hrw.org/news/2000/02/29/war-crimes-chechnya-and-response-west

Russian firepower aimed at chechnya's rebel fighters

Chechnya -- Chechen women and men pass by a Russian armoured personnel carrier in front of the destroyed presidential palace in Grozny. Feb1996[31]

---

[31] https://pressroom.rferl.org/a/revisiting-the-first-chechen-war/26735670.html

4 STATE TERRORISM

Remembering the 9/11 terrorist attack

State terrorism is when a government does not obey the law and doesn't give its people full human rights. As mentioned earlier, this was seen during the French Revolution of 1789. The revolutionary government in France had sent many people to their death, which was estimated at 30,000 people. Anyone who opposed the government was caught and often executed without a fair trial, by the guillotine. The motive of this was to control the people and to destroy any opposition so that the government would not be overthrown.[32]

Terrorism has also been used as a necessary tactic in a larger war. Terrorism in war is normally the killing of civilians (non-military) such as the Atomic Bomb drop on Japanese cities of Hiroshima and Nagasaki at the end of World War II. As mentioned above, the bomb killed over 200,000 civilians, the reason for this was to end the war as Japan wasn't going to surrender and thousands of allied lives would be lost if an invasion of Japan were to take place. However, calling this terrorism is debatable as every other

---

[32] French Revolution (Internet Website - Wikipedia, the free encyclopedia)
http://en.wikipedia.org/wiki/French_revolution#Reign_of_Terror

terrorist attack and in war; the US would say that they had good reasons for dropping the bomb but nonetheless this was an attack on civilians.[33]

There have been other attacks similar to this such as the Allied 'carpet bombing' of German cities during World War II which devastated cities and killed thousands. The aim was to destabilise the country, make them give in and to end the war in Europe. Some might say that even recent events such the US bombing Iraq during the Iraq war could be seen as terrorism as it killed many thousands of civilians.[34]

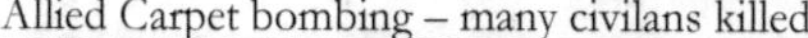

Allied Carpet bombing – many civilans killed

---

[33] Hiroshima (Internet Website - Wikipedia, the free encyclopedia)
http://en.wikipedia.org/wiki/Hiroshima

[34] Strategic Bombing (Internet Website - Wikipedia, the free encyclopedia)
http://en.wikipedia.org/wiki/Strategic_bombing_during_World_War_II

Fearsome: A Lancaster bomber in action during the Second World War

It is said that the Lancaster bombers that killed 600,000 in German cities had deliberately targeted civilians.[35] In addition, the German bombing of London during the 'blitz' was also seen as being a terrorist act on the civilian population of the UK.

---

[35] http://www.dailymail.co.uk/news/article-1216788/Did-Lancaster-bombers-killed-600-000-German-cities-deliberately-target-civilians-A-new-book-says-YES-.html

German bombers over the UK - Stukas in formation in April 1940. Stukas terrorised servicemen and civilians across Europe.

The Luftwaffe carried out raids on British urban targets for two months prior to the start of the Blitz, with the loss of over 1,000 civilian lives.[36]

---

[36]http://www.bbc.co.uk/history/events/germany_bombs_british_towns_and_cities

Many civilians killed and property damaged in the UK from German bombing

The former regime of Saddam Hussein in Iraq has been accused of state terrorism and repression to its own people. Under his regime people weren't allowed human rights and any opposition parties were trampled. Some would argue that this isn't terrorism because the government should be able to rule their country how they choose to; however it can be said to be another form of state terrorism as it is unlawful use of violence on civilians.[37]

Infamously, Iraqi dictator Saddam Hussein used sarin against Kurds in the town of Halabja in 1998, when his war planes dropped bombs containing the nerve agent. It killed 5,000 people immediately, and a reported 12,000 in the ensuing days and months.[38]

Another example of state terrorism is in the rainbow warrior incident. The Green Peace protest against the French nuclear tests in the Atoll region in 1985 led to the French Government to authorise the sabotage of the Greenpeace vessel (Rainbow Warrior), causing death among the crew.[39]

---

[37] Peter Hough, Understanding Global Security, Routledge, 2004, p63.
[38] http://www.dailymail.co.uk/news/article-4384652/The-Nazi-death-gas-horrific-Hitler-feared-using-it.html
[39] Rainbow Warrior (Internet Website - Wikipedia, the free encyclopedia) http://en.wikipedia.org/wiki/Sinking_of_the_Rainbow_Warrior

French military divers attached mines to the Rainbow Warrior to thwart Greenpeace protests against nuclear bomb tests on Mururoa Atoll in the Pacific.

French secret service agents bombed the 'Rainbow Warrior'. One crew member, Fernando Pereira, died in the explosion.

https://lematin.ma/express/2016/-rainbow-warrior--de-greenpeace-fera-escale-a-tanger/256273.html

American State Terrorism (Rogue Nation by its actions)

As the biggest proliferator of terrorism across the world – this superpower is acting like a rogue state.

In 2016 the USA had dropped 26,171 bombs.[40] The US was dropping nearly three bombs every hour, 24 hours a day. The majority of these attacks were in Iraq and Syria, but bombs were dropped in Afghanistan, Libya, Yemen, Somalia and Pakistan (all majority-Muslim countries).

Drone strikes were authorised by President Obama - he spread the use of drones outside the declared battlefields of Afghanistan and Iraq, mainly to Pakistan and Yemen. President Obama had labelled all males as combatants so that were allowed to be targeted by US drones, he had authorised at least 10 time more drone strikes than his predecessor George Bush.[41]

---

[40]America dropped 26,171 bombs in 2016. What a bloody end to Obama's reign - https://www.theguardian.com/commentisfree/2017/jan/09/america-dropped-26171-bombs-2016-obama-legacy

[41] Ibid

US President George W Bush

George Bush in his presidency had authorised the bombings – amounting to 70,000 bombs – US forces had attacked targets in countries that it was not at war nor had any ongoing conflicts, such as Pakistan, Somalia and Yemen.

US President Barack Obama

During President Barack Obama's reign (nobel Peace prize winner), over 100,000 bombs were dropped in seven countries. In his presidency he managed to drop 30,000 more bombs than president Bush done including two more countries. 563 strikes (mainly bu UCAV/drones) – countries such as Pakistan, Somalia and Yemen attacked.

US President Donal Trump

The current US president Donald Trump is deemed to surpass his predecessors in the numbers of bombs dropped and people killed by his authorisation.[42] According to the Pentagon's numbers give the following average:

George Bush's 8 years – an average of 24 bombs dropped per day (8,750 per year).

Barrack Obama's time in office – an average of 34 bombs were dropped per day (12,500 per year).

Donald Trump's (First year in office) – an average of 121 bombs dropped per day (44,096 per year). Hence, five bombs are dropped per hour - That averages out to a bomb attack at every 12 minutes.[43]

---

[42] Donald Trump Is Dropping Bombs at Unprecedented Levels - https://foreignpolicy.com/2017/08/09/donald-trump-is-dropping-bombs-at-unprecedented-levels/

[43] Every 12 Minutes, the United States Drops a Bomb Somewhere - https://www.thenewamerican.com/usnews/foreign-policy/item/29382-every-12-minutes-the-united-states-drops-a-bomb-somewhere

US F-15 Eagles strike aircraft dropping bombs

This is a massive loss of lives and destruction caused by 'trigger happy and war mongering US presidents with the full blessings of its military-industrial complex. According to the Pentagon, they are running out of bombs and plans to invest $20 billion in new munitions.[44] In addition, it has been estimated that the Pentagon has an unaccountable budget of $21 trillion spent on various defence procurements.

According to Witney Webb, a journalist said, **"Shockingly, more than 80 percent of those killed have never even been identified and the C.I.A.'s own documents have shown that they are not even aware of who they are killing—avoiding the issue of reporting civilian deaths simply by naming all those in the strike zone as enemy combatants."[45]**

---

[44] The US is running out of bombs — and it may soon struggle to make more - https://www.defensenews.com/pentagon/2018/05/22/the-us-is-running-out-of-bombs-and-it-may-soon-struggle-to-make-more/

[45] Trump's Military Drops a Bomb Every 12 Minutes, and No One Is Talking About It - https://www.truthdig.com/articles/trumps-military-drops-a-bomb-every-12-minutes-and-no-one-is-talking-about-it/

US troops in Afghanistan

It is easy for the US to state that all hit in a strike zone are enemy combatants – but in reality the vast majority are just civilians caught up in the attack. To kill an enemy combatant the US is recklessly killing anyone within the vicinity of the target. This type of attacks is 'state terrorism' on a vast scale. It seems that all US administration are not accountable to anyone for these atrocities committed – it's really a tantamount to war crimes.

US B-52 on a bombing run

US Sophisticated B1-B bomber displaying its firepower

According to Lee Camp (Lee Camp is an American stand-up comedian, writer, actor and activist. Camp is the host of the weekly comedy news TV show "Redacted Tonight With Lee Camp" on RT America.), **"Do you know where they're hitting? Who they're murdering? Why? One hundred and twenty-one bombs a day rip apart the lives of families a world away—in your name and my name and the name of the kid doling out the wrong size popcorn at the movie theatre"**.[46]

He further says, **"We are a rogue nation with a rogue military and a completely unaccountable ruling elite. The government and military you and I support by being a part of this society are murdering people every 12 minutes, and in response, there's nothing but a ghostly silence. It is beneath us as a people and a species to give this topic nothing but silence. It is a crime against humanity"**.[47]

---

[46] Ibid

[47] Trump's Military Drops a Bomb Every 12 Minutes, and No One Is Talking About It - https://www.truthdig.com/articles/trumps-military-drops-a-bomb-every-12-minutes-and-

Armed US UCAV (Drone)

Armed drone with laser guided bombs and Hellfire missiles

At last, it appeared that Pakistan's long-standing policy of supporting a Taliban front to establish a friendly, if not client, regime in Afghanistan that could provide strategic depth and quell its own ethnic (Pashtun and Baluchi) nationalist forces in Pakistan had borne fruit. However, the

no-one-is-talking-about-it/

successful results achieved by the Taliban had resulted in increasing tensions with neighbouring Iran, which could lead to further conflict in the area.

In 2001 the US had invaded Afghanistan as part of its 'war on terror' operation. Over 40 countries, including all NATO members. The aim was to dismantle Al-qaeda and remove the Taliban from power. The Taliban were quickly defeated in the initial invasion but later reorganized and launched an insurgency against the Afghanistan government and ISAF forces in 2003. The conflict in Afghanistan also spilled into Pakistan's borders and its Tribal areas, causing widespread security issues for Pakistani Government and its Armed Forces.[48]

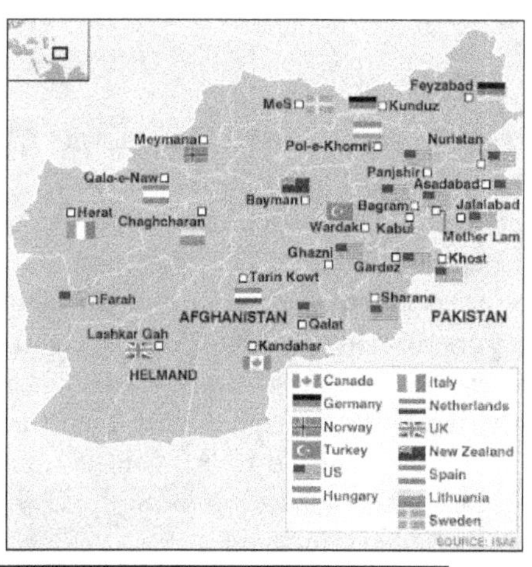

US troops began to increase from 2009-2011, reaching approximately over 100,000 and another 40,000 foreign troops under ISAF. Hence a total number of 140,000 troops were engaged with the rebel forces in Afghanistan. On the 1st May 2011, US Navy SEALS had allegedly killed Osam bin Laden in Abbotabad, Pakistan and in May 2012 an exit strategy was endorsed by NATO forces and

---

[48] Walsh, Eric (2017). Trump speaks with Afghan leader, U.S. commander calls for more troops'. Reuters.

many troops were withdrawn. By 2017 there were over 13,000 troops remaining in Afghanistan to support the Afghanistan Government. The War in Afghanistan is currently the longest war in United States history. Many thousands of people have been killed in Afghanistan – including over 4,000 ISAF soldiers and contractors, 15,000 Afghan security forces and over 31,000 civilians.[49]

US Soldier in Afghanistan

Despite the massive amount of military and economic aid that the US and its allies have poured into Afghanistan – it has not achieved the results it had desired. Afghanistan continues to be an unstable country with no signs of the conflict ending. The Taliban forces are thought to be occupying 40-70% of the country. The Pakistani government has rebuffed on many occasions by the US and Afghanistan governments accusation that Pakistan is giving sanctuary to the Taliban forces in its own country – Pakistan has stated that if the Taliban occupy more than 40% of Afghanistan, then they do not require any sanctuaries. Pakistan has suggested to Afghanistan and the US to clean its own 'house' up before making false accusations. If the

---

[49] Crawford, Neta (August 2016). 'Update on the Human Costs of War for Afghanistan and Pakistan, 2001 to mid-2016' (PDF).

US and its military might cannot stabilize Afghanistan and defeat the Taliban, then it's not fair if Pakistan is made to be the scapegoat for their inadequacies and failures.

US Troops in Afghanistan

According to the BBC news, **"Taliban fighters, whom US-led forces**  **spent billions of dollars trying to defeat, are now openly active in 70% of Afghanistan. Months of research across the country shows that the Taliban now control or threaten much more territory than when foreign combat troops left in 2014"**. [50]

---

[50] Taliban threaten 70% of Afghanistan, BBC finds (January 2018) - http://www.bbc.co.uk/news/world-asia-42863116

Taliban fighters

Taliban fighters

Pakistan's relationship has been tense on many occasions, especially with the presence of Indian security forces in Afghanistan – who are here on the pretext of helping and developing Afghanistan. Pakistan's see the Indians as

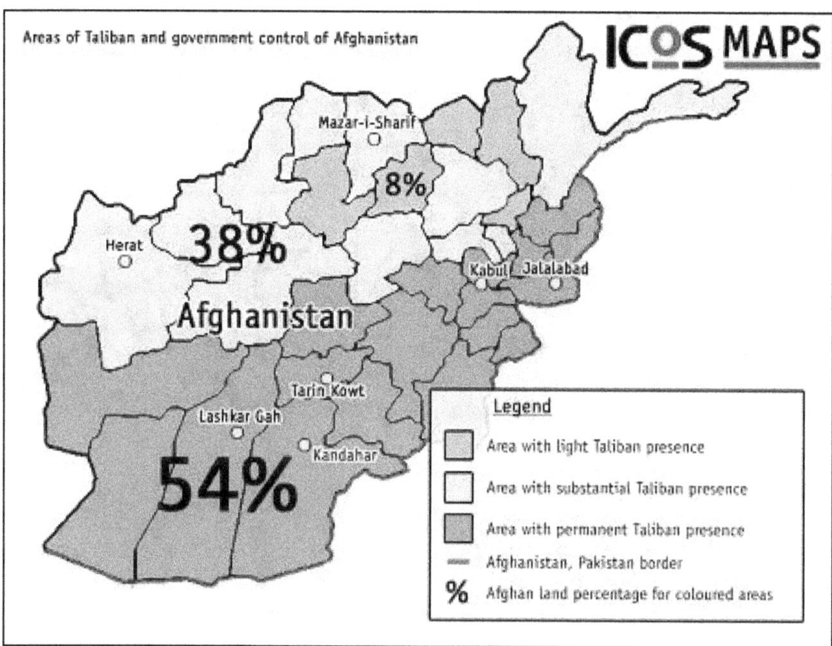

opening another front on its western border and supporting terrorist militant groups such as the TTP and other anti-Pakistan affiliates. Border clashes have on numerous occasions contributed to more tense relationship with Pakistan. The border fence that Pakistan is putting up with Afghanistan will reduce the number of militants and terrorists to enter Pakistan's porous borders. Pakistan has stated that to end the conflict in Afghanistan has to be a political solution – talking with the Taliban. Afghanistan President Ashraf Ghani on 28 February 2018 has stated, **"that Kabul is ready for talks with Pakistan, adding that they want to forget the past and start a new chapter"**. He further said, **"the peace process and a ceasefire must be agreed upon and that Taliban must be declared a political group"**. This is something that Pakistan has been trying to convince the US and Afghan governments that to end the conflict can only happen via a political solution.[51]

---

[51] Want to forget past and start new chapter with Pakistan, says Ashraf Ghani - https://www.geo.tv/latest/184054-want-to-start-a-new-chapter-with-pakistan-ashraf-ghani

German ISAF soldiers on patrol in Afghanistan

With US as being the sole global superpower and with the support of the largest and powerful global military alliance, NATO – the war in Afghanistan has come to a stalemate. This frustration and for the US it has become its longest war ever, it has unfortunately tried to scapegoat Pakistan for its own failures.[52]

---

[52] INDEX ON AFGHANISTAN, NATO FAILURE: A WINTER'S TALE, PART II - http://indexresearch.blogspot.co.uk/2008/03/index-on-afghanistan-nato-failure.html

Afghanistan –the America's Longest War

Pakistan and US Relations (America's War on Terror and its Impact on Pakistan)[53]

President Donald Trump and his administration has threatened tougher action in Afghanistan and had accused Pakistan of not 'doing enough' to contain the threat in Afghanistan. His remark on Twitter in January 2018 showed his hostility with Pakistan not doing enough to contain the conflict in Afghanistan. Afghanistan has been America's longest war so far – over 17 years of conflict since its 'war on terror' campaign. Pakistan was initially coerced into the 'war on terror' by

---

[53] http://www.politifact.com/truth-o-meter/article/2017/aug/21/donald-trumps-afghanistan-address-fact-checked/

the US - the Bush administration threatened to bomb Pakistan "back to the stone age" after the September 11 attacks if the country did not cooperate with America's war on Afghanistan. [54]

Former Pakistani Chief of Army - General Pervez Musharraf

General Pervez Musharraf and President George W Bush

---

[54] Bush threatened to bomb Pakistan, says Musharraf -
https://www.theguardian.com/world/2006/sep/22/pakistan.usa

US B2 Stealth Bomber, dropping its bombload onto a designated target

US B2 Stealth Bomber (PGM)

According to the former president, General Pervez Musharraf, the message was delivered by Richard Armitage (Assistant secretary of State) in conversations with Pakistan's intelligence director. He states the following, **"The intelligence director told me that (Mr Armitage) said, 'Be prepared to be bombed. Be prepared to go back to the stone age',"** [55] This shows the preparedness of a so called ally to coerce Pakistan — after 17 years of conflict in Afghanistan the US frustration has led it scapegoat Pakistan as the reason for the US and NATO's failure to defeat the Taliban

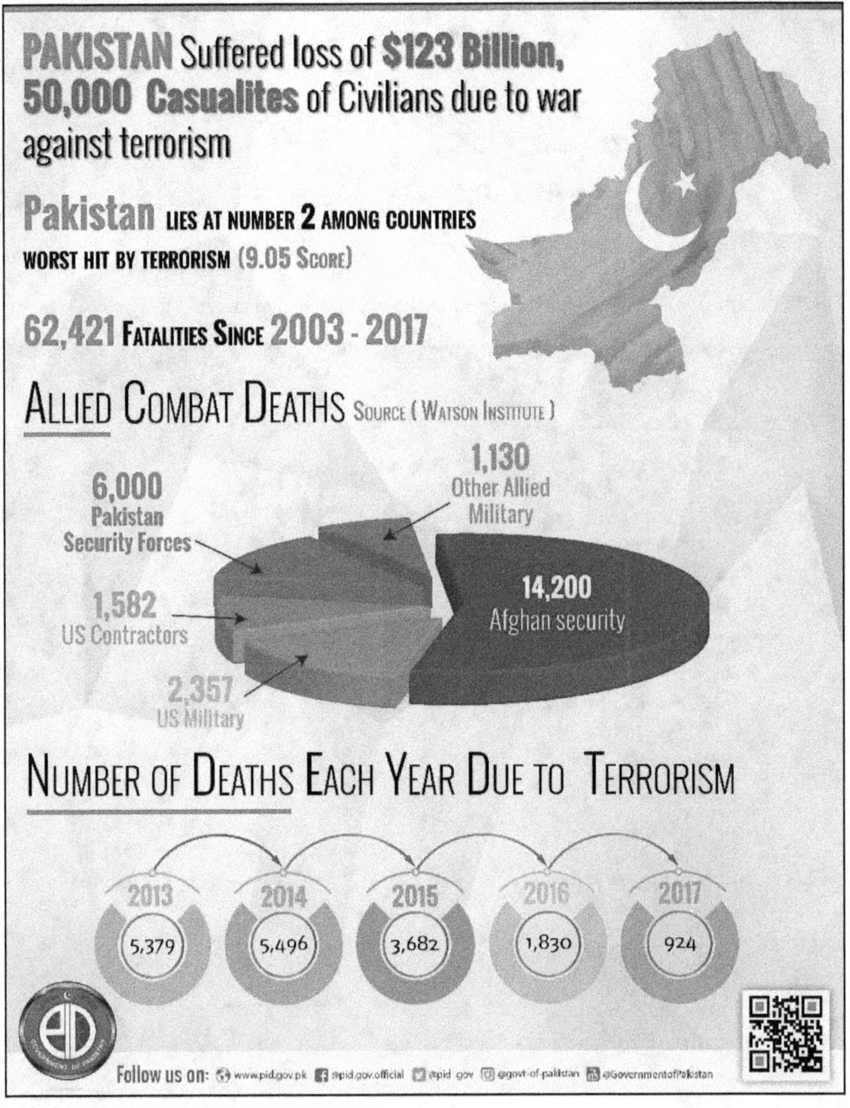

---

[55] Ibid

in Afghanistan. Pakistan has allowed the use of its territory to supply US/NATO and other international troops in landlocked Afghanistan, silently accepted American drones over its airspace, and co-operated with Western intelligence agencies against some terrorist groups like Al Qaeda. However, this has not been enough for the US – the US has threatened and rebuked Pakistan on a number of occasions and had established closer ties to Pakistan's nemesis India.

Richard Armitage (US Assistant secretary of State)

Pakistan has suffered from numerous drone strikes and has lost the largest number of civilians in America's war on terror. Pakistan lost over 50,000 civilians[56] in war on terror, and billions of dollars of economic loss. The US led war on terror has caused considerable resentment across the world and primarily in Pakistan – especially in the light of ingratitude from the US and its allies. The war on terror has led to many terrorist activities taking place and much loss of life. The Pakistan armed forces had waged a counter-insurgency war against terrorist outfits who were being supported by external powers to weaken and divide Pakistan.

---

[56] Pakistan lost 50,000 Civilians - https://tribune.com.pk/story/1599831/1-pakistan-lost-50000-civilians-war-terror/

Drone strikes by the US has caused widespread loss of innocent civilian lives and has led to widespread protests in Pakistan, resulting in tense relationship with Pakistan.

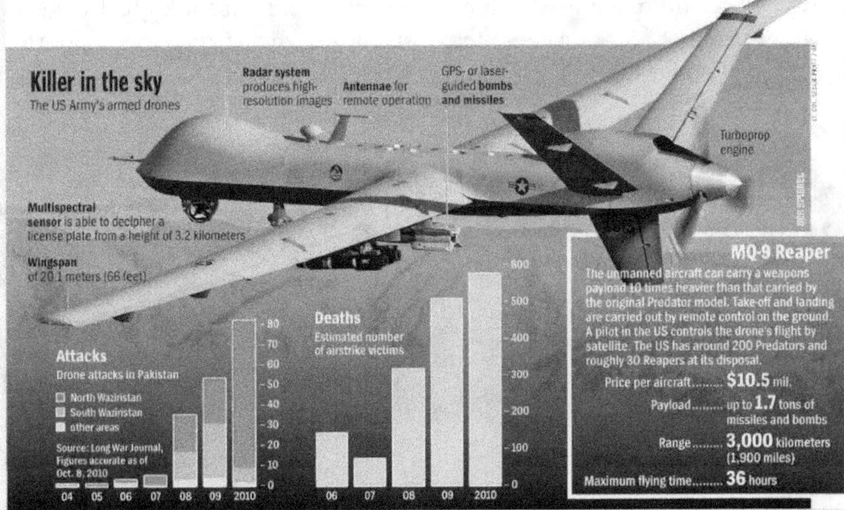

The intense and reckless drone attacks on the borders of Pakistan has contributed to further instability in the region. The loss of civilian lives due to drone attacks has caused a lot of ill feelings towards the US and its allies. The immoral weapon has been aptly used in developing countries and has violated numerous countries sovereignty.

Pakistan has stated that will shoot down any drone that violates its territory. The Pakistan Air Force (PAF), Air Chief Marshal Sohail Aman has warned that Pakistan would shoot down US drones if they violate its airspace.[57]

Operation Zarb E Azab (Counterinsurgency)

Pakistan has faced major threats to its security from terrorist incidents as a result of the conflict in Afghanistan (war on terror) – terrorist armed with heavy weapons and supported by foreign powers to cause maximum chaos and destruction of mainland Pakistan, with the aim of breaking the state of Pakistan as it is.

PAF F-16 Combat aircraft

Pakistan undertook operation Zarb E Azb and all three services of the armed forces of Pakistan played significant part in eradicating the terrorist threat. The PAF was employed to take out key strategic terrorist hideouts, but was wary of causing collateral damage. The PAF utilized its assets and precision strikes were initiated by the PAF fighter jets – F-16 Falcons, Mirages and JF-17 Thunders took part in the attacks on terrorist positions.

---

[57] http://www.paf.gov.pk

PAF JF-17 Thunder multi-role combat aircraft

This was the first time that the JF-17 thunder was employed in combat

PAF Mirage combat aircraft

roles – Turkish, Chinese and USA electronic pods were used (Sniper, Aselpod etc.). The PAF's JF-17's have probably used unguided and guided precision munitions – Laser guided bombs (LGB) may have been paired with the Chinese WMD-7 targeting pod. The various militants positions were tracked in the different regions close to the Afghanistan border.

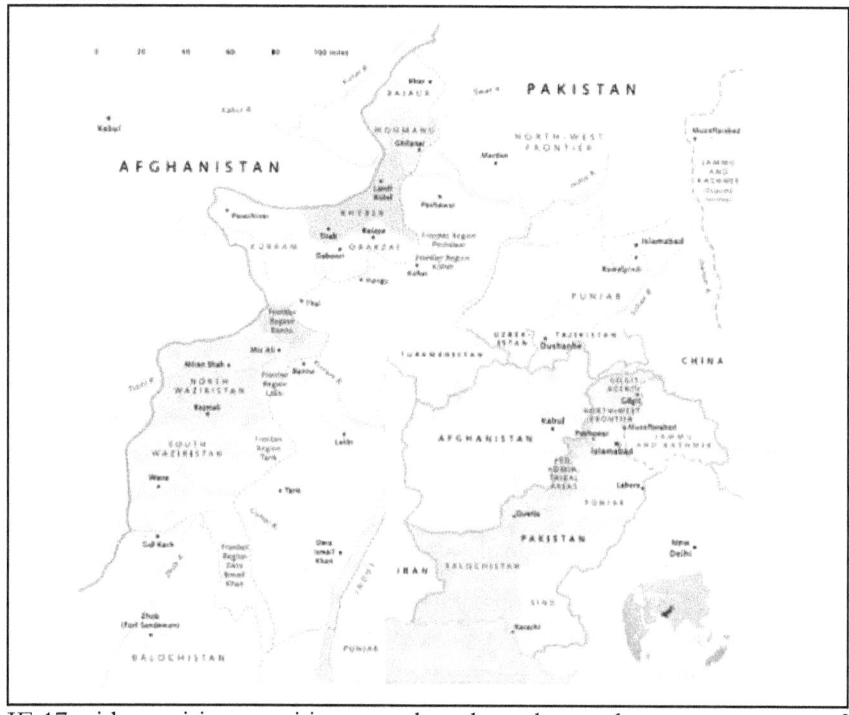

JF-17 with precision munitions are thought to have taken part on some of the attacks on terrorist positions in conjunction with PAF F-16s.

The aircrafts have operated with other air platforms in the PAF's inventory, such as its AWACS type aircraft and specially modified transport aircraft, such as the C130 Hercules aircraft.

The C130 were modified with FLIR equipment to track and locate enemy positions. They were working on an Intelligence, Surveillance and reconnaissance (ISR) mission.

The C130 would provide the target information and the PAF's jet fighters (including the JF-17) would partake in the strike missions.[58]

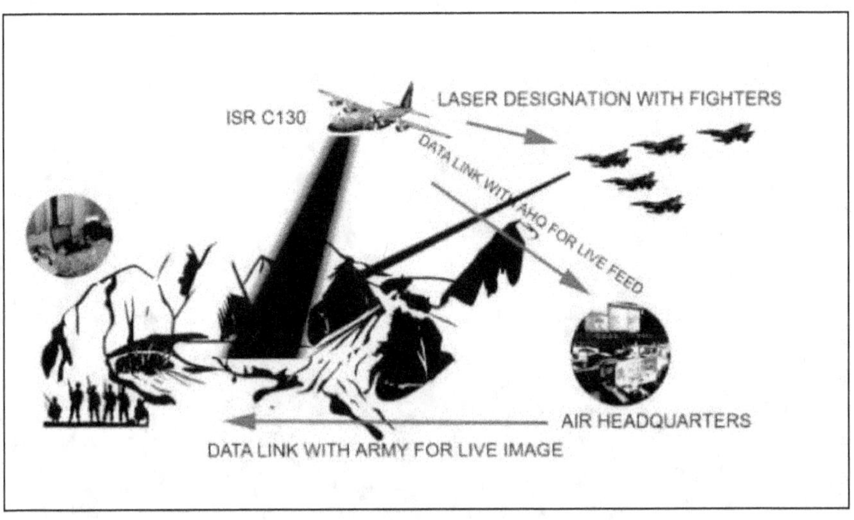

The combination of supporting aircraft with fighter aircraft has enabled the PAF to play a vital role in reducing and eliminating the serious threats to Pakistan's integrity. The terrorist violence has been significantly reduced as compared to many years back when the attacks were done on a daily basis

---

[58] http://www.paf.gov.pk

with a collosal loss of life and property. The JF-17 has taken part in many exercises in Pakistan and in China where its capability has been refined and made better after evaluations.[59]

A pair of armed PAF JF17 on a training sortie (Promotional video) PAF[60]

Combat missions

All in all, Pakistan has been aggressively using air power in its military campaign against terrorists in the country's restive northwestern regions along Afghanistan's border. The PAF combat aircraft in conjunction with the Pakistan Army's gunship helicopters have been pounding terrorist positions across the restive borders with Afghanistan.

As can be seen, the JF-17 had played vital roles in its own going security operations against terrorist outfits – such as Raad-ul-Fisaad and Zarab- i-Azab.[61] There is no doubt that as the aircraft matures and is incrementally upgraded, it will take on more responsibilities with a potent air defence and strike abilities.[62]

---

[59] http://www.paf.gov.pk

[60] https://www.youtube.com/watch?v=ZthdDd1Qj6A

[61] https://nation.com.pk/30-Dec-2017/paf-achieved-big-successes-in-2017

[62] https://warisboring.com/this-is-the-ultimate-mig-21-715bb9297261#.9t4jtsv29

PAF AWACS aircraft

Pakistan- US Relations

Pakistan's relations with the US appeared to be weakening following its nuclear tests and subsequent US missile attack on Afghanistan. The US has indicated that it expects Pakistan to unconditionally sign the CTBT and withdraw its support of the Taliban. On the other hand, Pakistan is anxious for the US to relax its punitive sanctions imposed after the May 28th tests. However, the US attacks on Osama bin Laden raised further Pakistani concerns regarding the methodology of the United States war on terrorism.[63] All in all, the US pressures on Pakistan and the attempt to cause instability in Pakistan has resulted in ties being at the very low end. Drone strikes, military and economic blackmail and a threat to Pakistan on a terrorist list has not helped with the relationship. The fear for Pakistan is a new assertive and Zionist influenced US trump administration and its close nexus with Israel and India – is seen as a recipe for potential conflict. Pakistan's fear of

---

[63] Umer Farooq, Striking Consequences, Janes Defence Weekly, September, 1998, Pg23

a nexus of powerful non-Muslim countries are trying to divide and destroy Pakistan under the pretext of the 'War on Terror'. Pakistan is keeping a good watch on the ways that the destruction of Muslim majority countries have taken place, Such as in Iraq, Libya, Syria etc.

A fully armed US MQ-9 Reaper UCAV

US Drone strike on militants on the Afghanistan and Pakistan border

US Accused of 'Violating Pakistani Sovereignty' in Taliban Drone Strike

Drone strikes killed more civilians than publicly acknowledged' – UN investigator[64]

The Objectives of foreign powers are to destabilise Pakistan through a number of methods, such as its development projects. The aim is to weaken Pakistan's position on the international front and allow Indian hegemony in this part of the globe.

---

[64] https://www.rt.com/news/un-drones-report-afghanistan-us-366/

A number of tactics are being used by Pakistan's adversaries:

- Use of non-state actors
- Proxy wars (ethnic conflicts to be engineered)
- Encourage and Support local unrest
- Intensification of Propaganda war (Fake news/Psychological warfare)
- Target and undermine political leadership
- Use all opportunities to cripple the nation and put military and political pressure
- Attempt to undermine economy and project nation as a 'failed state'
- Attack the nations cohesion and encourage divisions amongst its populations.
- Give public platform to extremist and terrorists in Pakistan (international propaganda of an independent separatist/terrorist movement such as the BLA)
- Multi-pronged attacks from all directions – Information and Cyber warfare, Attack on its culture, bogus human rights issues to be intensified, global political pressures by intense lobbying and blackmailing, encouraging residency to the US of corrupt and 'traitorous' people such as the former Pakistani ambassador to the USA, fund and increase criminality, terrorism, proxy wars, continue to encourage and support corrupt regimes/governments in Pakistan etc.
- Intense 'fake news' channels and websites to a negative global limelight and hence an excuse to undertake any international interventions in the future.
- Scapegoating Pakistan's for all the ills plaguing the US and its allies in the South Asian region.

A brief look at some of the tactics used against Pakistan:

The Ethnic conflicts

Encouraging and supporting ethnic conflicts In Pakistan. India with the support of its allies is encouraging and fomenting unrest in the aim of destabilising and weakening Pakistan. Terrorist such as the BLA, BLF have been given sophisticated arms to wage war on the Integrity of Pakistan.

There are numerous evidence of proof that Indian RAW, with US CIA, Afghanistan KGB are supplying weapons to these terrorist groups, especially with development of the Gwadar port (a collaboration with China and Pakistan)/CPEC project that is viewed as a significant investment in Pakistan's development.

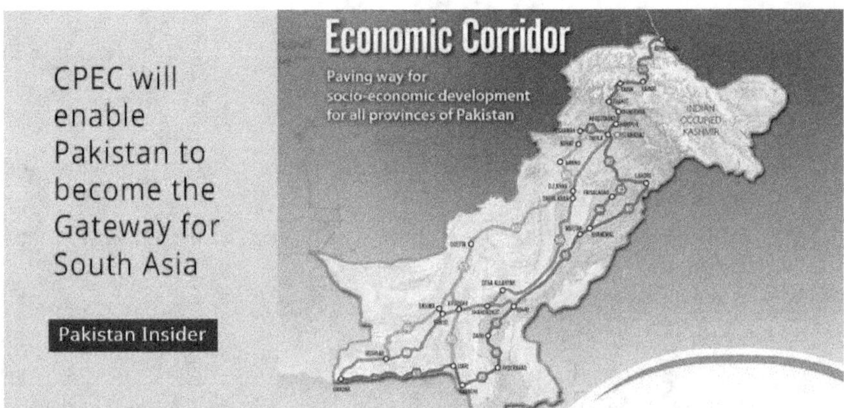

Gwadar CPEC Pakistan

India's investment In Afghanistan is used as a pretext to undermine neighbouring Pakistan. It is giving an opportunity to destabilize Pakistan and create a major rift between the two Muslim countries. In addition, the funding of RAW to a political party in Pakistan (MQM) is a further proof of this attempt to cause instability.[65]

The Sectarian Divide

The Sunni-Shia rivalry has been exploited by a number of countries for their own vested interests. Pakistan has the largest number of Shia population after Iran. There have been many sectarian attacks in the country with the aim of initiating a sectarian conflict – divide and conquer scheme. Traditionally Saudi Arabia and Iran's competition for leadership of the Muslim world has resulted in these countries supporting and sponsoring havoc in Pakistan. The aim of increasing the sectarian divide has on the whole failed so far – due primarily to the strong military's dealing with this threat.

Pakistan's adversaries are using and exploiting any means to cause disharmony and internal conflict. Evidence of this has been found amongst a number of foreign intelligence agencies operations in Pakistan. The sectarian card will also benefit Iran who currently have strong ties with India's Hindu fundamentalist government of Prime minister Modi. Iran is allowing India to develop0 the Chabar sea port in direct competition to Pakistan's Gwadar project. Also tension on the Iranian and Pakistani borders have on occasions intensified with a number of fatalities on both sides. An Iranian spy drone was shot by the PAF in 2017.

International Isolation

There has been an attempt in isolating Pakistan on an international level, India has spearheaded in this direction and other countries such as the USA have also attempted to do this. For the USA, it is extremely upset and humiliated that the War in Afghanistan has cost them trillions of dollars and so far its longest serving war of 17 years with no result of 'winning' this war. Despite this duration, the USA with Afghan forces only occupy 40% of the territory, the remaining 60% is in the hands of the Taliban. The USA inability to defeat the Taliban have led them to scapegoat Pakistan for their own failings.

---

[65] Anam Sheikh (2017), India's hybrid warfare in Pakistan -
https://www.globalvillagespace.com/indias-hybrid-warfare-in-pakistan/

The only superpower with the most powerful military alliance (NATO) has not been able to defeat the Taiban and hence attribute this to the Pakistani's. The Pakistan government has recommended that a military victory is not achievable and that negotiations with the Taliban would be fruitful for all – however the American led 'ego' is unable to see this and is bent on 'teaching' Pakistan a lesson. It has attempted to put Pakistan on the terrorist sponsoring nations and with India is trying to undermine the integrity of the nation.

India has attempted to malign Pakistan's image, especially with the Hindu fundamentalist prime minister Modi wooing of foreign powers about Pakistan's alleged terrorism support. The Kashmir freedom struggle is being tarnished as a terrorist support, when in actually it has been a freedom struggle from Indian occupation. Intense Indian and Zionist lobbyists in Washington have started to cause major friction between Pakistan and USA. Indian Prime minister Modi and US President Trump declaring Sayeed Salahuddin as a terrorist was an attempt at weakening Pakistan's case on Kashmir. Negative view of Pakistan is predominantly given on Indian and Western Media – psychologically undermining Pakistan's credibility to the average person.[66]

The pseudo-liberals and Religious extremists

Pakistan also faces an insidious threat from the Pseudo-Liberals (some have been promoting Islamophobia) and religious extremists (with their own brand of wrong religious thought). These two groups have tried to eradicate the real Islamic Identity Of Pakistan – a Muslim Identity of mainstream Islam (the middle way, not too lose or too extreme). They have attempted to confuse and divide the nation – Pakistan has a number of ethnic groups and provinces, the only thing uniting them is their Islamic ideology. Pakistan's adversaries are trying their best to cause divisions within this area and have supported both sides to cause disharmony in the country – this would weaken Pakistan and its adversaries will an hedgemonistic control of this country. [67]

Political Standoff

---

[66] Anam Sheikh (2017), India's hybrid warfare in Pakistan -
https://www.globalvillagespace.com/indias-hybrid-warfare-in-pakistan/

[67] Ibid.

Pakistan also faces aspects of a US inspired regime change to ensure a compliant political leadership, which has no commitments to Pakistan's self-interest. To do this, US foreign policy is to actively promote the political fragmentation and Balkanization of Pakistan as a state. Us desires a Pakistani leadership that will serve its global hegemonistic ambitions.[68] It intends to weaken the central government and cause divisions amongst the federal structure. The US has had access to various military bases in Pakistan and has used the 'war on terror' as the pretext for this – US Special Forces are expected to vastly expand their presence in Pakistan as part of training and counter-terrorism units.

The Balkanization of Pakistan

A Yugoslav-like fate was predicted by the US National Intelligence Council (NIC) and the US Central Intelligence Agency (CIA) in 2005. It was predicted that the country would in a civil war like scenario, inter-provisional rivalries and much bloodshed. Pakistan was deemed to become a 'failed state' with complete Talibanisation and lose its control of its nuclear weapons.[69] For Pakistan this was a sign that foreign powers were trying to 'engineer' this kind of scenario and were utilising all means of carrying out their plans of 'splitting Pakistan into different pieces – balkanization of Pakistan'.

Pakistan began to take appropriate measures to ensure that this foreign engineered plan did not materialise. Accordingly to the NIC and CIA scenario, "Pakistan will not recover easily from decades of political and economic mismanagement, divisive policies, lawlessness, corruption and ethnic friction,"[70] The US and its allies (including Israel and India) had planned to encourage social, ethnic and factional divisions with the aim of the territorial breakup of Pakistan. The US strategy was to redraw the borders Iraq, Iran, Syria, Turkey, Afghanistan and Pakistan. According to professor Michel Chossudovsky, **"This US agenda for Pakistan is similar to that applied throughout the broader Middle East Central Asian region. US strategy, supported by covert intelligence operations, consists in triggering ethnic and religious strife, abetting**

---

[68] Prof Michel Chossudovsky (2012), The Destabilization of Pakistan - http://www.globalresearch.ca/images/harita_b.jpeg
[69] Prof Michel Chossudovsky (2012), The Destabilization of Pakistan - http://www.globalresearch.ca/images/harita_b.jpeg
[70] Ibid,

and financing secessionist movements while also weakening the institutions of the central government".[71]

US F-35 releasing a laser guided bomb (PGM)

Pakistan's Oil and Gas reserves

According to the Pakistani Petroleum Ministry advisor Zahid Muzaffar, Pakistan's shale gas and oil reserves are more than the combined reserves of Central Asian States put together.[72]

---

[71] Ibid.
[72] https://tribune.com.pk/story/998520/oil-and-gas-sector-pakistans-reserves-more-than-all-central-asian-states/

'Pakistan's reserves more than all Central Asian states

Pakistan has extensive sources of oil, gas and untapped mineral resources, especially in its Baluchistan province. It has a number of projects that caused considerable interest from its adversaries – who do not want a strong economic and stable Pakistan. Economic prosperity will further enhance its defensive and offensive capability and would 'check mate' and potential threat from its enemies.

- Baluchistan province comprises over 40% of Pakistan's land mass
- Pakistan is thought to have an estimated 25.1 trillion cubic feet (Tcf) of proven gas reserves of which 19 trillion are located in Baluchistan.
- Pakistan had proven oil reserves of 300 million barrels (according to the Oil and Gas Journal) and other estimates are six trillion barrel of oil reserves - most of which are located in Baluchistan.
- Potential Iran-Pakistan pipeline corridor (also to include India if relationship improves) is poised to transit through Pakistan's Baluchistan province
- Gwadar deep sea port (financed by China) will give access to China and other countries of the supplies of Oil/Gas and other goods. This would improve the economic prospects for Pakistan and

ensure a new trading route to a number of countries, including Central Asia.

Gas reserves discovered in Khairpur[73]

Covert Support to Baluchistan militants

Pakistan's Baluchistan province has seen evidence of foreign sponsored aid to militants who are trying to separate or breakaway from Pakistan. The militant leaders have been given refuge in India and western countries and indicate the levels of support from these areas. There is evidence that the US and its allies (CIS, KHAD,RAW etc.) are trying to woo and foment troubles in this region. Sophisticated arms are being provided to these misguided militants (a tiny segment of these militants are causing problems).

Professor Michel Chossudovsky says, **"The stated purpose of US counter-terrorism is to provide covert support as well as as training to**

---

[73] https://www.pakistantoday.com.pk/2016/01/16/gas-reserves-discovered-in-khairpur/

"Liberation Armies" ultimately with a view to destabilizing sovereign governments. In Kosovo, the training of the Kosovo Liberation Army (KLA) in the 1990s had been entrusted to a private mercenary company, Military Professional Resources Inc (MPRI), on contract to the Pentagon. The BLA bears a canny resemblance to Kosovo's KLA, which was financed by the drug trade and supported by the CIA and Germany's Bundes Nachrichten Dienst (BND)".

Baloch population in Pink: In Iran, Pakistan and Southern Afghanistan

There is evidence that foreign countries including the USA are favouring the dismemberment of Pakistan's Baluchistan province into a 'greater Baluchistan, which would also incorporate the Sistan province in Iran'. This would to territorial loss for Pakistan and Iran. The war on terror is helping the US and its allies engineer a breakup of Pakistan – It is also making it difficult for it to get favourable international loans it needs to help it stabilise economically. The US has influenced IMF and other global financial institutions of putting more indirect pressure that could cause the central government to collapse, thereby not having the ability to allocate resources to the federal governments. The potential is for the federal governments to be unhappy and more chances of it being influenced by external agencies to break away and ensure the loss of Pakistan's territorial integrity.

There have attempts by the US to study on ways of splitting Pakistan up – a study undertaken by US Lieutenant Colonel Ralph Peters in 2006 (writing for 'The Armed Forces Journal') showed this and became further evidence of the US's thought process in engineering the dismemberment of Pakistan. Pakistan should be broken up, leading to the formation of a separate country - Greater Baluchistan or Free Balochistan (incorporating the Pakistani and Iranian Baloch provinces into a single political entity).

Furthermore, Pakistan's North West Frontier Province (NWFP)/Khyber Punktunwa should be incorporated into Afghanistan "because of its linguistic and ethnic affinity". This proposed fragmentation would reduce Pakistani territory to approximately 50 percent of its present land area and also loose a large part of its coastline on the Arabian Sea.. Even though the map does not officially reflect the US Pentagon's doctrine, it is thought to have been used in many training programs for senior military officers.[74]

---

[74] Prof Michel Chossudovsky (2012), The Destabilization of Pakistan - http://www.globalresearch.ca/images/harita_b.jpeg

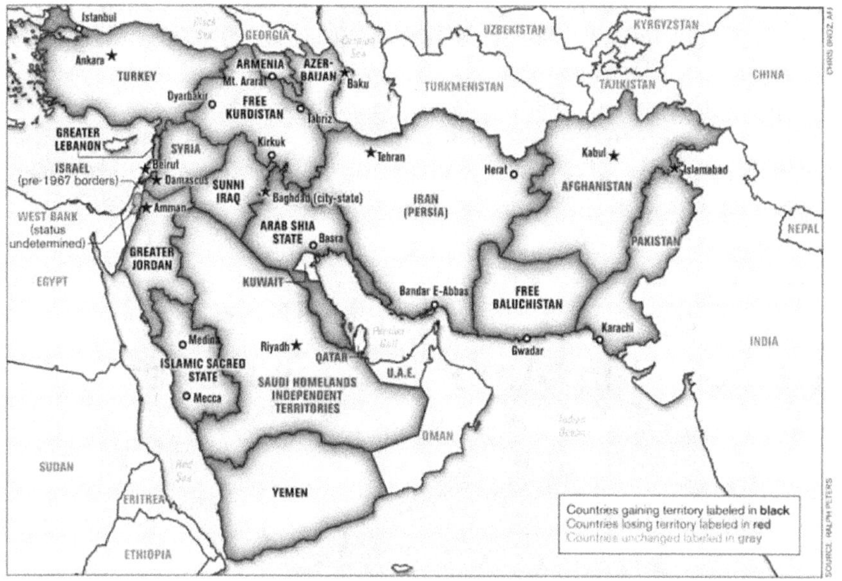

Other influential papers are also calling for the Balkanization of Pakistan, the Huffington Post with the sub-heading of 'breaking Pakistan to Fix it', states the following, **"The argument for Balkanizing Pakistan or, more specifically, fragmenting the Islamic Republic so it's easier to police and economically develop, has been on the table since Pakistan's birth in 1947.... And lately, the concept is looking more appealing by the day, because as a result of flawed boundaries combined with the nexus between military rule and Islamic extremism, Pakistan now finds itself on a rapid descent toward certain collapse and the country's leaders stubbornly refuse to do the things required to change course. But before allowing Pakistan to commit state suicide, self-disintegrate and further destabilize the region, the international community can beat them to the punch and deconstruct the country less violently".[75]**

---

[75] Michael Hughes, Balkanizing Pakistan: A Collective National Security Strategy - https://www.huffingtonpost.com/michael-hughes/balkanizing-pakistan-a-co_b_635950.html

In 2012 an American congressman, Dana Rohrabacher (Republican of California) proposed a bill that called for the secession of Pakistan's largest province, Baluchistan. Dana Rohrabacher, stated that the people of Baluchistan, a sprawling western province racked by a seven-year-old separatist insurgency, should "have the right to self-determination and to their own sovereign country." This resulted in a furious response from Pakistani politicians and media, with Prime Minister Yousaf Raza Gilani calling it an attack on Pakistani sovereignty.[76]

US should support independent Balochistan: American lawmaker

PTI | Oct 13, 2017, 20:25 IST

Tickets Start From 40 AED

Watch Dolphin & Seal Show In Our Fully Air Conditioned Indoor Facilities

HIGHLIGHTS

- Congressman Dana Rohrabacher said Pakistan needs to remember what happened in 1971, referring to developments in then East Pakistan which later on became Bangladesh.

- "The Baloch are also persecuted, mainly persecuted by the Pakistanis who have them under their thumb, and they murder people constantly," he alleged.

Rohrabacher said the Muhajirs do not want to be subjugated by "this corrupt, militaristic, pro-terrorist" government of Pakistan.

https://twitter.com/national_baluch/status/918911146220032000

The Pakistani's have accused Mr. Rohrabacher of seeking to "balkanize" Pakistan and that the USA is attempting to put pressure on establishing

---

[76] New York Times (2012) Fury in Pakistan after US congressman suggests that a province leaves
http://www.nytimes.com/2012/02/22/world/asia/fury-in-pakistan-after-us-congressman-suggests-that-aprovince-leave.html

covert listening posts on the border with Iran. The Pakistanis feel that the senator was acting at the behest of American intelligence agents. In 2011 a border incident in which US helicopters deliberately targeted 2 Pakistani posts in which led to 24 Pakistani Soldiers being killed, though the US disputed on details of the border clash. For Pakistan, this was another way of putting military and psychological pressure on Pakistan if it did not comply with US desires.[77]

Helicopters used in US/NATO led attack on 2 Pakistani border posts

---

[77] New York Times (2012) Fury in Pakistan after US congressman suggests that a province leaves
http://www.nytimes.com/2012/02/22/world/asia/fury-in-pakistan-after-us-congressman-suggests-that-aprovince-leave.html

Attack helicopters were used to kill 28 Pakistani border soldiers in a deliberate attempt to send a message to Pakistan.[78]

Funeral for the Pakistani soldiers killed from US led NATO attacks on its border troops

---

[78] US helicopters kill 28 Pakistani troops on Afghan border - https://www.longwarjournal.org/archives/2011/11/us_helicopters_kill.php

<u>Maps Redrawn - Pakistan Fears for the Worst</u>

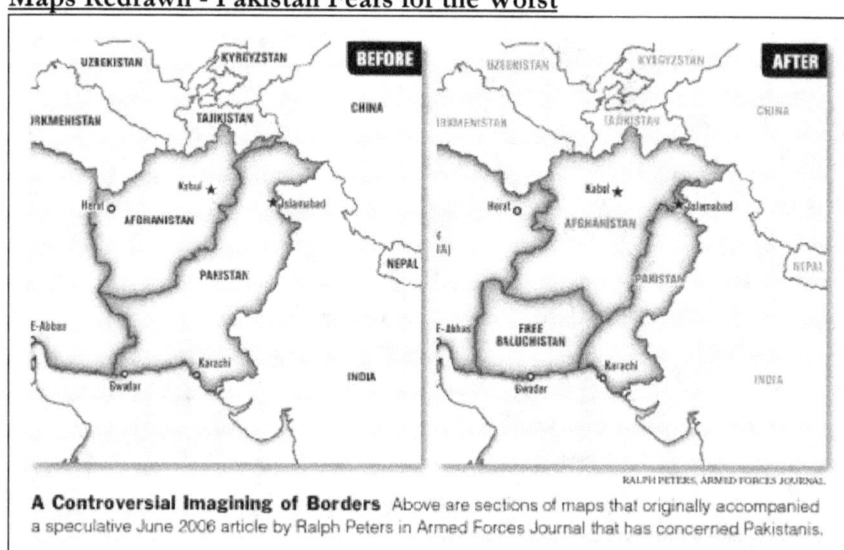

A Controversial Imagining of Borders Above are sections of maps that originally accompanied a speculative June 2006 article by Ralph Peters in Armed Forces Journal that has concerned Pakistanis.

The above map and the various statements from US congressman and the negative media propaganda against it (primarily in India and the Western World) has led to Pakistan feeling betrayed by the US and has fueled a belief that that the United States really wants to breakup Pakistan. Pakistan fears, that the US in collaboration with Afghanistan, India and covert Zionist support from Israel are attempting to destroy Pakistan. The recent US tilt towards India has further corroborated these beliefs.[79]

Brigadier Asif Haroon Raja, states the following, **" The US ignores its own human rights violations and also looks the other way to massive human rights abuses committed by Israel, India, Egypt and other dictatorial regimes towing its agenda. Washington, however, has no tolerance for democratic regimes that refuse to make their countries compliant States and opt to pursue independent foreign policy best suited for their national interests. Various excuses are manufactured to bring suchlike defiant States in line. The more often dirty tactics in use are sanctions, orchestrated political turmoil and chaos, coercion, threats, proxy war, psychological operations, propaganda, regime**

---

[79] New York Times, Maps Redrawn , Pakistan Fears for the Worst -
https://mt360.wordpress.com/2008/11/24/maps-redrawn-pakistan-fears-the-worst/

change, and if needed, physical assault and occupation of targeted country".[80]

He further states, " **The Indo-US-Israel nexus is adept in contriving a false narrative to build a case against a country. Going by the dictum of Joseph Goebbels, the trio repeatedly utter lies and half-truths to convert falsehood into truth and convincing the audience to accept black as white. The targeted ruling regime is demonized and discredited under a well-planned media campaign to justify intervention and a regime change".[81]**

Brigadier Asif Haroon Raja

Brigadier Asif Haroon Raja, further highlights the US and its allies tactics in the region, **"Since 9/11, the US has used proxies, terrorism, sedition, propaganda war and coercive tactics as tools to destabilize the targeted country. It has meddled in internal affairs of Afghanistan,**

---

[80] Brigadier Asif Haroon Raja, Pakistan Tribune (2018) USA's treacherous agenda against Pakistan - http://paktribune.com/articles/USAs-treacherous-agenda-against-Pakistan-243339.html

[81] Ibid.

Iraq, Syria, Libya, Tunisia, Egypt, Sudan, Somalia, Chad, Turkey, Iran and Pakistan. All are Islamic countries and their peoples are all Muslims". [82]

Historically Pakistan has a long time ally relationship with the US, but at critical times it was let down. The US under the influence of strong zionist lobbies in the USA have drastically focused primarly on the Muslim world and have gradually caused divisions and destructions of the countries in the region – one by one it is attempting to weaken and destroy all countries that have the potential to be strong and assertive.

Accordingly, Brigadier Asif Haroon Raja states, **"The second Afghan war that immediately followed the 9/11 brought back Pakistan in the good books of the US and it was quickly made a non-NATO ally. This was, however, a deception since Pakistan was in reality a target and was to be destabilized, denuclearized and Balkanized covertly. After brewing up war on terror in FATA, Khyber Pakhtunkhwa and Baluchistan, Pakistan was subjected to cooked-up allegations that it was in cahoots with the militants and that its nukes were unsafe. The hidden objective of the US was exposed in 2006 after the publication of an article in US Defence Journal titled "Blood Borders" written by Lt Col Ralph Peters. The map showed changed boundaries of Middle East, and Baluchistan a separate state".** [83]

---

[82] Ibid.

[83] Ibid.

Furthermore, he argues, **"The 'Do More' mantra introduced in 2005/06 was meant to brew political stabilization, bleed economy and foment insecurity. Indo-US-Israel-Western media campaign demonized Pakistan that it's Army and ISI were supporting terrorism. Idea was to discredit the Army, brand Pakistan a terror abetting State and Pak Army/ISI rogue outfits. A narrative was built that Pakistan was collapsing, nuclear arsenal was unsafe and its nukes might fall into wrong hands (Islamic extremists). Objective was to give an excuse to USA to declare Pakistan a failed State and to occupy Islamabad and the provinces of Punjab, Sindh and Baluchistan and seize nuclear arsenal".**[84]

For Pakistan there has been a number of schemes for the country to be destablised. A senior Indian Navy officer Commander Kulbushan Yadhav was caught in Pakistan's Baluchistan province. He was travelling under the false name of Mubarak Hussain Patel and had been operating since 2003 at the Iranian Chahbahar port. He was given substantial money by India's RAW intelligence agency (allegedly upto $400 million) to plan and carryout a number of destablising and terrorist attackes in Pakistan. He and his handlers/workers were supplying weapons to the Baluchi terrorists (BLA etc.), gaining knowledge of Pakistan's Makran-Karachi seacoast for future amphibious landings, evidence of supplying money to the MQM mohajir party in Pakistan's Sind province, scare the chinese from investing in Gwadar sea port, Scuttle CPEC development.

---

[84] Brigadier Asif Haroon Raja, Pakistan Tribune (2018) USA's treacherous agenda against Pakistan - http://paktribune.com/articles/USAs-treacherous-agenda-against-Pakistan-243339.html

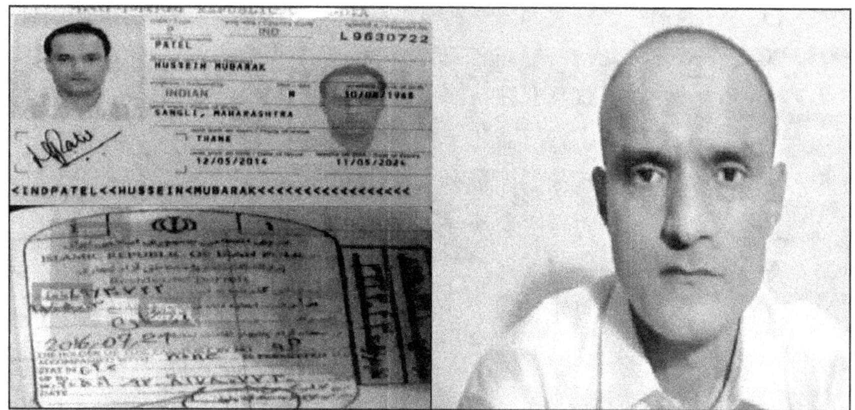

Indian Navy officer Commander Kulbushan Yadhav formenting terrorism in Pakistan

The USA was also thought to be supplyimng arms and attempting to antogonise the Pakistani population bordering afghanistan by contnuosly doing drone strikes so that they rebel against the central government (via CIA and Blackwater). The aim was to cause divisions between the civilian

and military populations. It is alleged that NATO containers were also used for supplying arms.[85]

Brigadier Asif Haroon Raja – The US needs to do more[86]

Pakistan is one of few countries that its population see as the only institution that is not corrupt like its Civilian counterparts. It has high esteem for its armed forces, and hence the aim was to dilute and cause friction between the support of the people for its armed forces. The US had spent considerable amount of money in its operations in Baluchistan, according to Christina Fair (an American academic that has fervour of hatred against Pakistan and this is seen by many being on the payroll of foreign agencies) thye US had pumped in more money in Baluchistan than in Iran and yet has failed to make it independent.[87]

Pakistan has established even closer strategic relationship to its ally China and is making mends its realtionship with Russia. It is seeing the threats of destablisation and eventual balkanization of Pakistan's territorial integrity by 3 'axis of evil' – USA, India, Israel (zionist lobbies and indo-Israeli nexus) and a puppet Afghanistan government. All of these 'axis of evil' are influencing the US administraion and its allies to attack and strike Pakistan. It is looking for more excuses and is continually asking Pakistan to 'do more' mantra – Pakistan has started to reject these allegations and plans and

---

85 Ibid.
86 https://www.youtube.com/watch?v=MGjQAGfVUOs
87 Ibid.

has asked the USA to do more in its conflict on War on terror in Afghanistan.

Brigadier Asif Haroon Raja further states, **"Since August 22, 2017, he and senior US leaders have adopted a highly belligerent posture against Pakistan. Series of threatening statements have been issued and Pakistan put on notice. Pakistan's response that it has done enough and will not do any more, and that it is now the turn of USA and Afghanistan to do more is rational and logical. It has rightly rejected the US paltry aid, stressing it needs respect and acknowledgement of its sacrifices, and adding that it can keep fighting terrorism at its own without American assistance. Pakistan has discontinued military cooperation and intelligence sharing with USA, and has other effective options to exercise in case the US opts for a unilateral punitive action. Pakistan's principled stance seem to have mellowed down the jingoism of hawks in USA and they have started giving reconciliatory feelers".[88]**

The above are considered to be 4th generation wars, evolving to Hybrid wars on Pakistan. Many analysts have mentioned the threats that Pakistan is facing internally and externally. The folowing manp indicates the growing pressures that Pakistan has been put in.

PAF Combat aircraft

---

[88] Ibid.

Hybrid Warfare on Pakistan

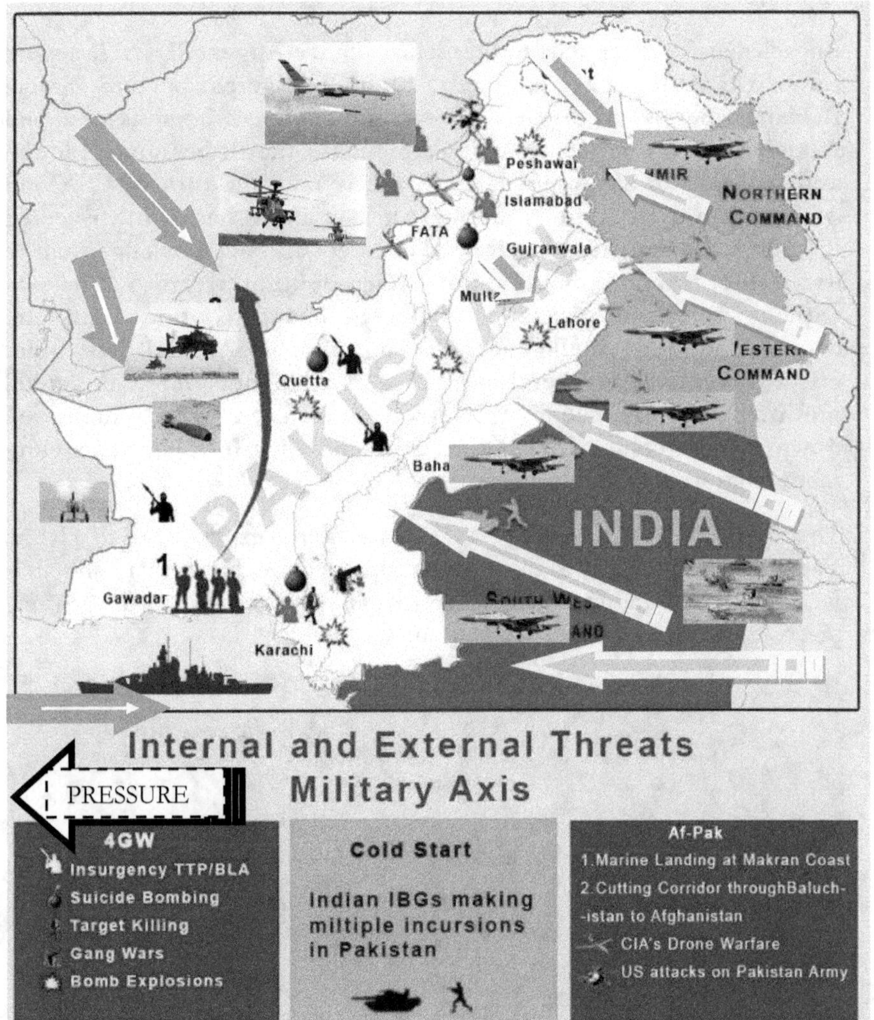

4G Warfare, Cold Start, Af-Pak deployed against Pakistan (modified map)[89]

---

[89] 4G Warfare, Cold Start, Af-Pak deployed against Pakistan -
http://www.brasstacks.pk/
https://forum.bodybuilding.com/attachment.php?attachmentid=5204213&d=135
6182812

The phrase **'axis of evil'** is used against countries that are accused of sponsoring terrorism, seeking weapons mass destruction, causing instability and planning to do serious harm to a nations territorial integrity. The Phrase was initially coined by U.S. President George W. Bush in his State of the Union address on January 29, 2002. Currently Pakistan has the following 'axis of evil' countries that are trying their best to weaken and dismember Pakistan.

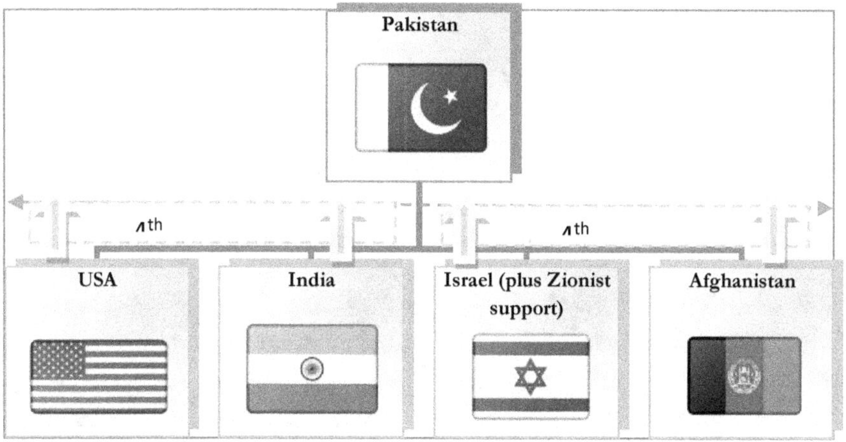

Pakistan's current 'Axis of Evil'

Pakistan has so far successfully thwarted the designs of its adversaries, but still has serious threats to deal with on all fronts. It has successfully carried out a number of operations to eradicate internal terrorist threats and to reduce external influences. The Director General of Inter Services Public Relations (ISPR) Major General Asif Ghafoor announced that Pakistan Army has successfully completed Operation Khyber-4. [90]The results of the operations were as follows:

---

[90] Samaa.tv (2017) Pakistan Army successfully completes Operation Khyber-4 - https://www.samaa.tv/pakistan/2017/08/pakistan-army-successfully-completes-operation-khyber-4/

- Scores of landmines were defused by the troops in the operation.
- Operation Khyber-4 was carried out with strong and complete planning - Every single terrorist in Rajgal and Shawal was targeted.
- Clearance operation had taken place in Khyber Valley, where 91 security checkposts have been set up.
- The military had consultation with NATO forces during the operation.
- Security forces have carried out 3300 operations under Radd-ul-Fasaad so far. In addition, Pakistan's 'Rangers had carried out 1728 operations across its Punjab province.

Summary

The above case studies were to highlight the different ways that states embark on a journey of coercion, bullying and outright direct state sponsored terrorism or through the use of its proxy assets. Pakistan was discussed in a deeper detail to show the various ways that powerful countries such as the USA are causing deliberate destabilising of nations via a number of ways – which many will consider as nothing short of terrorism.

Pakistan Army Cobra gunship helicopters used against foreign sponsored TTP and related terrorist groups

5 TERRORISM IN WARS OF LIBERATION

US Soldier: "The Real Terrorist Was Me And The Real Terrorism Is This Occupation"[91]

Terrorism can sometimes be used against governments, when people want to break free form a government, terrorism has been used to achieve their political aim. An example of this was the Rhodesian War (1972-1980). Rhodesia (now Zimbabwe) was an African country controlled by a white minority. There were two groups which used terrorism to fight to free the black community from both Britain and the white minority. Terrorism was used by these groups to frighten any black who worked for or helped white people to make it difficult for the white community to survive. The groups aim was to destabilize the country so that the whites would leave. This is considered terrorism as it is the use of violence to intimidate people but some would argue that it isn't because without using terrorism, the groups wouldn't be able to achieve their political aims.[92]

---

[91] https://themindunleashed.com/2015/05/us-soldier-the-real-terrorist-was-me-and-the-real-terrorism-is-this-occupation.html

[92] Rhodesian War (Internet Website - Wikipedia, the free encyclopedia) http://en.wikipedia.org/wiki/Rhodesian_War

Rhodesian Light Infantry prepare for airborne operations during the bush war[93]

Suspected black political activist being mistreated by troops of the white supremacist minority government in Rhodesia (Zimbabwe).

---

[93]https://www.reddit.com/r/MilitaryPorn/comments/2mbmcw/rhodesian_light_infantry_prepare_for_airborne/

Two white supremacist regimes in Africa – were South Africa and Rhodesia in which a minority white government was ruling over a majority black population. In the case of Rhodesia, in 1965 the UK broke its relationship with the country after it refused to recognise the white minority rule (who comprised 3.72 percent of Rhodesia's 1960 population). In Rhodesia (Zimbabwe) this led to a war between the white supremacist regime against a number of black resistance movements.[94]

The white supremacist regime had routinely employed terror/torture tactics (including electric shocks and skull bashing) in order to obtain information from suspected political activists. One of the black resistance groups was led by Robert Mugabe, who took control of ZANU and its military wing ZANLA – it had emerged as the strongest rebel group amongst many others. Eventually Robert Mugabe took control of the country from the white supremacist minority government. And became the president of the country.[95]

President Robert Mugabe of Zimbabwe (Rhodesia)

---

[94]https://medium.com/war-is-boring/why-white-supremacists-identify-with-rhodesia-480b37f3131f
[95] Ibid

Global terrorism

Global terrorism covers a wide range of terrorist actions which in some way have an effect on another state. There are many examples of this type of terrorism as there have been many terrorist attacks recently, predominantly in the Middle East. One example is the Israel-Palestine conflict. The dispute over land had resulted with the formation of the Palestinian Liberation Front whose aim was to return all occupied land back to the Palestinians

One of the terrorists/Israeli flag flies at half-mast at the Olympic stadium[96]

This dispute over land has led to many terrorist attacks against Israel. An example of this was the Munich Massacre when Palestinian militants broke into the Israeli compound at the 1972 Munich Olympics killing an athlete and a trainer. The militants took Israelis hostages. The Palestinians demanded the release of Arab prisoners held in Germany and a safe passage out of Germany. A rescue plan was ordered which resulted in the deaths of all the hostages (Israelis), Palestinians and a policeman. The reason terrorism was used was because it would put great pressure on the German authorities to give in to their demands or face many innocent casualties. Many people would say that this is terrorism but the terrorists would say

---

[96] www.digitaljournal.com/article/332098#ixzz5N90ijjP2

that this is the only way they will achieve their political aims.[97]

It is argued that Israel was born out of terrorism – as it wrested control of the country from the majority Palestinian population. It had committed a number of terrorist actions against the British who were the colonial powers at the time – in order to seek a separate country.[98] Due to the atrocities committed via the holocaust in Nazi Germany (in Europe) – the Zionist lobbies with the colonial powers at the time decided that a homeland for Jewish people should be made in another country called Palestine.

It is ironic that the atrocities committed against the Jewish people in Europe had resulted in them being rewarded a nation in someone else's country – in this case, in Palestine. Europe could have given the Jewish population a homeland within Europe or in America but chose to give them a country that they had no right of taking over. The Palestinian people have been kicked out of their own country/land by the then colonial great powers with the support of Zionist lobbies and its respective military wings. This has been the real cause of the Palestinian/Israeli dispute. Prior to the creation of Israel - Jewish and Muslim relationships had been extremely good.

Israel has been supported by a number of powers and has been provided a vast economic and military support over the many years since its creation in 1946. It has gradually began to wipe out the Palestinian identity and nation. It has received massive support from the US and its allies – vast military support, making it the most powerful country within the Middle East (with nuclear capability).

This vast Israeli capability and intense powerful Zionist lobbies across the world had made Israel one of the most powerful nations on the world. Daily Israeli propaganda against the Palestinians have enabled them to gain much support (mainly from western governments). In order to gradually eradicate Palestine from the world map, Israel has continued with a number of brutal tactics (state terrorism) on the Palestinian populations and at the

---

[97] Munich Massacre (Online, Wikipedia) http://en.wikipedia.org/wiki/Munich_massacre

[98] https://www.nam.ac.uk/explore/conflict-Palestine

same has coerced other large powers such as the USA (who have a very powerful Zionist lobbies), to gradually subdue and dismantle all the countries around it – Iraq, Syria, Lebanon, Jordan, Egypt, Libya etc.

It has continued with barbaric attacks on its Palestinian population and has allowed massacres to be taken place with its blessings, such as the case of Sabra and Shatila incident.

Sharon during the Yom Kippur War in 1973[99]

The former Israeli Prime Minister Ariel Sharon on 16-17 1982, had deliberately allowed a Lebanese Christian militia to attack a refugee camp (Sabra and Shatila), killing up to 2,000 Palestinians. He was forced to resign once it was established an Israeli investigative panel that had declared him to be personally responsible for this massacre. [100]

---

[99] http://www.france24.com/en/20140103-ariel-sharon-controversial-former-israeli-prime-minister-dies-age-palestinian

[100] Noam Chomsky (2014): Sabra & Shatila Massacre That Forced Sharon's Ouster Recalls Worst of Jewish Pogroms
https://www.democracynow.org/2014/1/13/noam_chomsky_sabra_shatila_massacre_that

Innocent Palestinian families were butchered at the refugee camps with Israeli permission.

Palestininans mourning the killing of loved ones

The tragedy of many innocent killed in this massacre – human depravity had reached new levels.

https://twitter.com/benfcampen

<u>Impact on human rights</u>

The US and its allies have given massive amount of military aid to Israel, despite its horrendous human rights record. Human rights violations have not been a primary barrier to weapons sales at any time in history. The world's nastiest dictators, tyrants, human rights abusers and anti-democratic governments have been the customers of all of the major arms supplying countries in the world and still continue to be so.

For instance, Israel is considered as one of the worst human rights abusing state across the Middle East region. There are ongoing tensions between Israel and its Palestinian population in the West Bank and Gaza part of the country. Since the formation of the Israeli State (on the former nation of Palestine), the Israeli government and its military has been at war against the Palestinian population, who are seeking to get their country back from

Israeli occupation.

A two-state solution has been proposed to resolve this intractable long term conflict – however, the right wing government of Benjamin Netanyahu has no real intentions of resolving this and just wants to usurp the Palestinian land and eradicate Palestinian history and culture. With a strong Zionist lobby across the world (especially the USA) it continues to deliberately tell a false narrative of its intentions for a peaceful resolution with the Palestinian population. It has continued to promote the Palestinians in a negative light and has continued to tarnish its reputation.

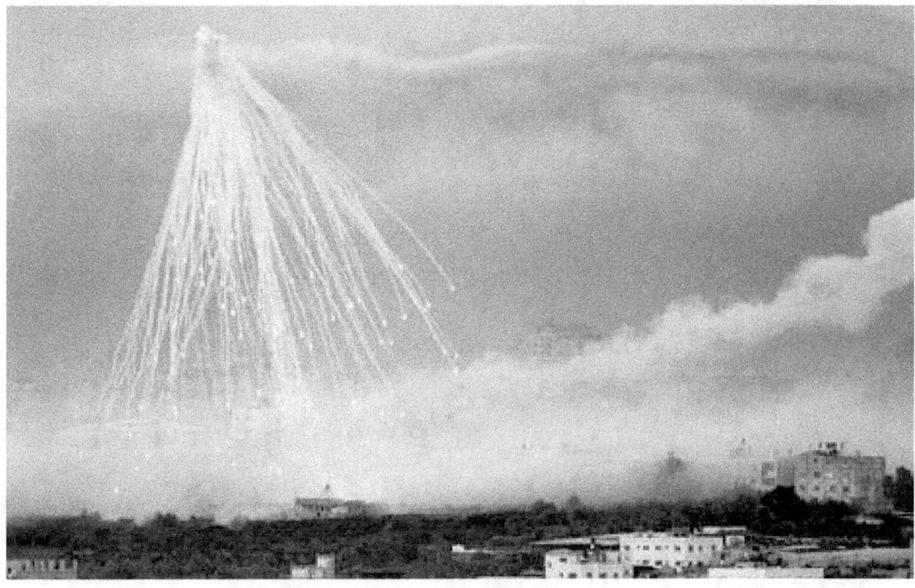

Israeli use of white phosphorus on the Palestinians has caused outrage and horrendous killings of the Palestinian population in Gaza.[101]

---

[101] https://www.flickr.com/photos/free_world/3223064725

Palestinians being subjected to an Israeli Phosphorus attack

Israeli Prime Minister Benjamin Netanyahu and his hardline policy on the Palestinian population. According to Human Rights Watch (HRW), this nothing more that war crimes committed by the Israeli State (state terrorism at its best). HRW states, **"Israel's repeated firing of white phosphorus shells over densely populated areas of Gaza during its recent military campaign was indiscriminate and is evidence of war crimes"**.[102]

White Phosphorus Use Evidence of War Crimes

Indiscriminate Attacks Caused Needless Civilian Suffering

(Human Rights Watch - HRW)

---

[102] Human Rights Watch (HRW) - https://www.hrw.org/news/2009/03/25/israel-white-phosphorus-use-evidence-war-crimes

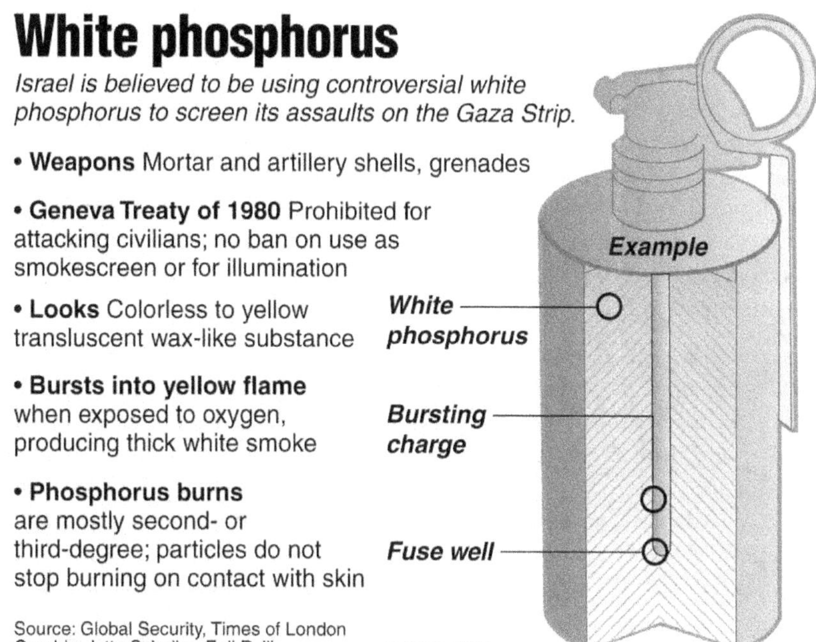

Some of the tactics undertaken by some Palestinians group have been ruthless on numerous occasions. They include bombings, kidnapping and extortion, but the Israeli response has been the systematic suppression of the Palestinian people. Since the outbreak of the conflict, many tens of thousands of Palestinian people have been killed, and millions have been displaced.

In May 2018 , the United Nations (UN), were outraged by continuous killing of Palestinian people by Israel. *'Enough is enough': UN condemns Israel as Palestinians bury their dead – video report*[103]. Israel has strong support from the Zionist lobbies across the globe and especially the USA and hence believes it is above the norms of international relations. There is widespread evidence to suggest that if the Israeli government does not resolve this conflict with the Palestinians then there could be a catastrophic conflict in the near future – this would not be in the interest of any as there will be further loss of lives. The cycle of conflict

---

[103] Guardian - https://www.theguardian.com/world/video/2018/may/15/enough-is-enough-un-condemns-israel-as-palestinians-bury-their-dead-video

would cause further hatred and hence insecurity in the country and the region at large.

Indo-Pakistan Border skirmishes and artillery duels

Indo-Pakistan tensions have existed since both countries achieved independence from British India. They have gone to war on a number of occasions and have had numerous border skirmishes and artillery duels. This has caused tensions to further flare up and loss of lives for the border troops as well as the civilian population on both side of the border. Many thousands have been injured over the years and this has caused more resentment from both sides.

Tensions have increased in Indian occupied Kashmiri where over 700,000 military/security personnel are suppressing the indigenous people of this part. Constant battles with local militants (who have local support of the people) and Indian security forces have intensified. There are numerous cases of genocide committed by Indian security forces (mass graves have been unearthed). The Indian's are using Israeli tactics in suppressing the local population. Israel continues to provide much expertise to its ally India in this area as it has tested these barbaric tactics to the Palestinian people over the many decades. In addition, fake news and false narratives are propagated by the Indian forces and media, and this has led to support from non-Muslim countries to the Indian cause. However, truth will always come out eventually and this is what is causing the Indian government, especially the fundamentalist BJP Hindu party of Prime Minister Modi a lot of issues. The attacks against Indian forces have been increasingly carried out by local militants, rebels willing to sacrifice their lives for freedom from Indian occupation and subjugation. The fear is that this region could lead to a catastrophic nuclear war between India and Pakistan if these issues are not amicably resolved.

Indian border troops

Pakistani border troops

Indian artillery men lift the turrets of the 155mm Bofors guns

Pakistani artillery men

Surgical strikes, nothing more than border skirmishes[104]

The analyst Riaz Haq (South Asia Investor Review) has stated the following, **"The essence of Kashmir issue today is not Uri or Pathankot or similar other alleged "militant attacks"; it is India's brutal military occupation force of 700,000 heavily-armed Indian**

---

[104] What Indian and Pakistani Newspapers Said About 'Surgical Strikes' Along Line of Control - https://blogs.wsj.com/indiarealtime/2016/09/30/what-indian-and-pakistani-newspapers-said-about-surgical-strikes-along-line-of-control/

soldiers being resisted by over 10 million Kashmiris. Anyone who tells you otherwise is a liar".
According to Riaz Haq, **"Not only is the Indian government denying the right of self-determination granted to Kashmiris by multiple UN Security Council Resolutions, New Delhi is also reneging on the commitments made by India's founder and first prime minister Jawaharlal Nehru to Kashmiris and the international community".**[105]

"...our assurance that we shall withdraw our troops from Kashmir as soon as peace and order is restored and leave the decision regarding the future of the State to the people of the State is not merely a promise to your Government but also to the people of Kashmir and to the world."

(Jawahar Lal Nehru, Telegram No. 25, October 31, 1947, to Liaqat Ali Khan, PM of Pakistan)

Indian Prime Minister Jawaharlal Nehru's Pledge[106]

Riaz further states, "India is deploying 700,000 troops with extraordinary powers to detain, torture, blind, injure and kill any Kashmiri citizen with impunity under Armed Forces (Jammu and Kashmir) Special Powers Act 1990".

There is widespread evidence and documentation of state sponsored violence against the Kashmiris in India. Dr. Angana Chatterji, a professor of cultural and social anthropology at California Centre for Integral Studies, stated that the **"violence and militarization in Kashmir, between 1989-2009, have resulted in over 70,000 deaths, including through extrajudicial or fake encounter executions, custodial brutality, and other means".** she further added. **"In the enduring conflict, 667,000 military and paramilitary personnel continue to act with impunity to regulate movement, law, and order across Kashmir,"** (The International Peoples' Tribunal on Human Rights and Justice).[107]

---

[105] 700,000 Indian Soldiers Versus 10 Million Kashmiris -
http://www.riazhaq.com/2016/09/700000-indian-soldiers-versus-10.html
[106] 700,000 Indian Soldiers Versus 10 Million Kashmiris -
http://www.riazhaq.com/2016/09/700000-indian-soldiers-versus-10.html
[107] Ibid

The many years of oppression in Indian occupied Kashmir has further contributed to the ill-feelings and desire of the Kashmiris to free themselves of Indian occupation of their land. New generation youngsters such as Burhan Wani and many others - who have only witnessed Indian occupation and repression against their people, have become more determined to resist the illegal military occupation of their land by India.[108]

Human rights activist Ajit Sahi has exposed on numerous occasions the atrocities in Kashmir committed by the Indian Prime Minister Modi's BJP fundamentalist government. Ajit Sahi says, "6 people a day being killed in extrajudicial killings". (Tom Lantos Human Rights Commission).[109] A lot of the suppression that the Indian army and security personnel have undertaken have been borrowed from the Israeli security forces in their brutality against the Palestinian people. Close military connection between Israel and India has increased significantly, with the support of sophisticated Israeli arms to quell any form of resistance in Indian occupied Kashmir. Many of the brutal tactics employed by the Indian army and security forces has been barbaric and have taken leaf from the Israeli expertise in subduing the Palestinian population. There are widespread evidence, of torture, mass rape committed by the Indian armed forces to humiliate and subjugate Kashmiri women. The use of rubber bullets/pellets and other extreme tools have caused widespread injuries and resentment amongst the Kashmiri population. India has used mass propaganda to project this as nothing more than 'terrorists' when evidence shows otherwise.

It is clear that these kind of suppression tactics will result in more Kashmiris taking up arms against the illegal Indian occupation of Indian held Kashmir.

---

[108] Ibid

[109] Human rights activist Ajit Sahi -
https://www.youtube.com/watch?v=CBjfOERnLz0

India has started to use the same brutal tactics as the Israeli armed forces have done to the Palestinian people[110] There is a close military alliance between these two countries.

Indian atrocities in Occupied Jammu and Kashmir

The systematic torture and human rights violations against the Kashmiri people in Indian occupied Kashmir has increased tensions between India and Pakistan. The Fear is that the brutal oppression in occupied Kashmir could become the catalyst for a major conflict with neighbouring Pakistan.

Brutal and heavy handed tactics by the Indian army/security forces (numbering over 700,000 troops) have further alienated the Kashmiri population – there are evidence of genocide (mass graves), torture, rape by Indian security forces, use of pellet guns blinding many people etc,

---

[110] India must stop crimes against humanity in IOK: Sardar Masood Khan, Kashmir Watch - http://kashmirwatch.com/india-must-stop-human-right-violations-and-crimes-against-humanity-in-iok-sardar-masood-khan/

- The Indian military forces are behaving like an occupying force and oppressing the basic human rights of the people in this area. [111]

Kashmir Death caused by the Indian Army

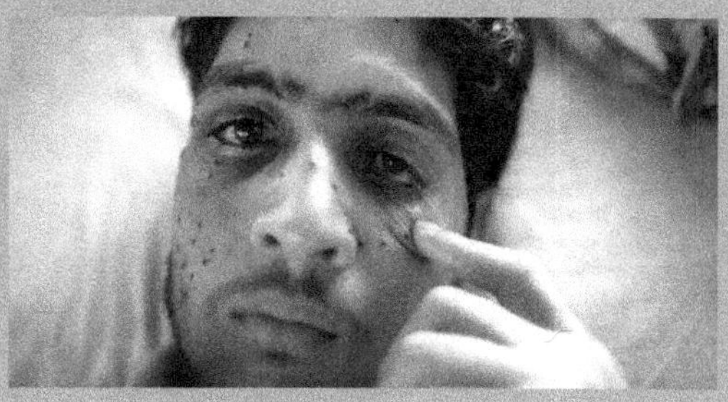

Pellet guns are deliberately used to blind protestors against the illegal occupation of Indian held Kashmir. There are cases of many individuals being blinded by these nasty weapons.

India has attempted to project these uprisings as terrorist movements when in fact it is no more than freedom movements to rid of Indian

Many cases of extra judicial killings, missing people, uncovering of mass graves, thousands of Kashmiri women being raped as a means of humiliation and subjugation, widespread use of torture under the pretext of fake militant encounters – all undertaken by Indian military and security forces. Despite repeated claims of being the largest democracy in the world – none of this has been given to the Kashmiri people in Indian held Kashmir. There are widespread evidence of

---

[111] Kashmir Conflict in Contemporary India - https://cafedissensusblog.com/2017/03/27/kashmir-conflict-in-contemporary-india/

oppression in Indian occupied Kashmir. India blames Pakistan for causing the issues, but in reality it fears that if the people of Kashmir are given their rights to decide (as per UN resolution) then the Kashmiris will either join with Pakistan or become totally independent. Kashmir should have naturally joined with Pakistan at independence – but India's invasion of Kashmir under the pretext of Hari Singh (Hindu Maharaja of Kashmir) request for help (which was requested when the people of Kashmir rebelled against the decisions of Hari Singh to side with India). The Muslim majority population was illegally seized by Indian forces and should have naturally joined with Pakistan at its inception..

Indian atrocities available to the global media – but India's propaganda machine has successfully washed away these concerns.

Evidence of mass rapes by Indian security forces in occupied Indian Kashmir has been documented by numerous human rights and government organisations.

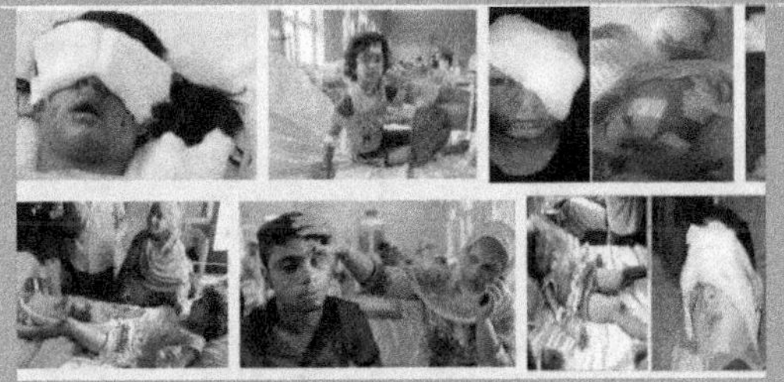

Evidence of torture and use of inhumane weapons to break the resistance movement in Indian held Kashmir. Due to India's rapid economic growth rates, foreign powers such as the USA and its allies have now started to turn a blind eye to these Indian atrocities and genocide being committed in this part of the world.

https://www.pinterest.co.uk/pin/393853929895656016/

Excessive use of torture and killings have further alienated the Kasmiri people in Indian occupied Kashmir. India has the world's largest number of troops in one area – over 700,000 soldiers are used to subdue the people in this area.

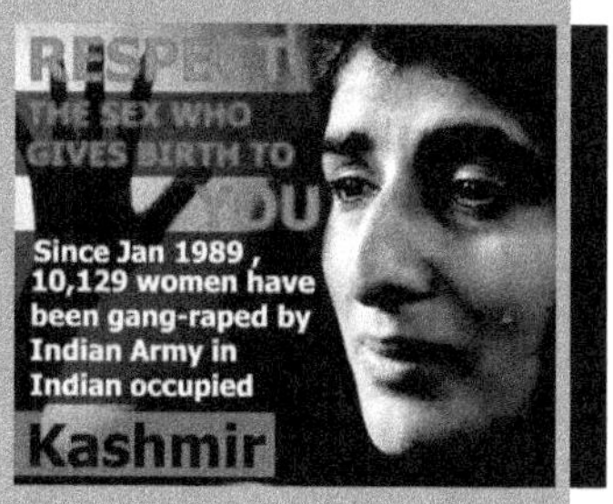

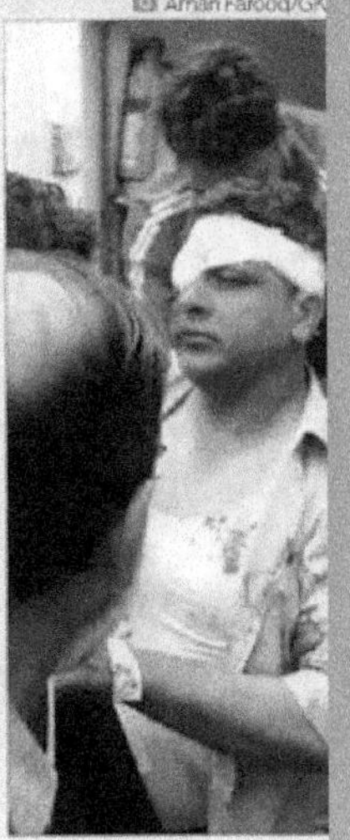

In 3 days, pellets 'darken world' of 100 youth

90% injured may lose vision in affected eye, fear SMHS doctors

ZEHRU NISSA

Srinagar, July 12: Ward No 8 at general specialty SMHS hospital here clearly reflects the agony of Kashmiri youth who have been hit by pellets by forces during street protests in the past four days. And the scale of injuries and injured is gruesome, according to medicos treating these patients at the Ward.

For the first time since the injured, mostly hit with pellets in face and eyes, started pouring in at this Ward, medicos are admitting that the situation is "extremely grave."

"We have never received so many pellet injuries in such a short span of time," a doctor at the Ward told *Greater Kashmir*. "The surgeons are working overtime to operate upon the injured."

Till Tuesday afternoon, 115 youth, mostly in the age group of 15-25, were admitted at the hospital with pellet injuries. Hospital authorities said 93 injured had been "already operated upon."

While officials claimed over 60 injured had been discharged after preliminary treatment, doctors said the story was "different."

» See **In 3 days**...on Pg-8

Kashmir;
Jan 1989 to March 2016
Total killings = 94,332
Custodial killings = 7,043
Civilans arrested = 133,387
Structures arsoned/ destroyed = 106,06
Women widowed = 22,810
Children orphaned = 107,556
Women gang raped/ molested = 10,17(
Enforced dis-appearances = 10,000+

According Inamul Haq, (Phd student of Central University of Gujarat, India), **"The basic reason for the breakout of the violence was the rigged elections of 1987, followed by an armed revolt after, and had drawn the Kashmir Valley into the conflict zone. The state was put under undeclared emergency from the 1990s, which disrupted the values of rule of law and made possible the violation of human rights and restricted the fundamental freedom of the people of the Valley. The law enforcement agencies suppressed the voice of self-determination by using force and creating alienation towards the Indian state. The popular uprisings in 2008, 2010, and 2016 prove this alienation. The prominent laws like AFSPA and PSA gave a free hand to security forces in propagating cruel and inhuman treatments on the people of Kashmir"**.[112]

And further states. **"From July 09, 2016, the uprising after the death of Burhan Wani should be a matter of utmost concern not only for India, but the whole world. The approach adopted by the Indian state is the evidence that for India, there is only value of Kashmiri resources and not Kashmiris............ The demand of plebiscite, the slogans of Azaadi (freedom), the rage of stone-pelting and the raising of Pakistani flags showed the isolation people felt from India. There are so many events that clearly show that people in the Valley do not want to remain a part of India. Why are the educated youth in Kashmir, unlike the earlier militancy movements, picking up arms?"**.[113]

---

[112] Kashmir Conflict in Contemporary India - https://cafedissensusblog.com/2017/03/27/kashmir-conflict-in-contemporary-india/

[113] Ibid

The disputed Kashmir has been the main bone of contention between India and Pakistan – majority of the issues between the 2 countries always are related to Kashmir region. Both sides need to amicably resolve this dispute and end the sufferings in this part of the world . India needs to adhere to its promise of giving the Kashmiris the right to self-determination that it had promised once it had invaded occupied kashmir at the behest of the Hindu Maharaja Hari Singh. The Hindu fundamentalist government of Prime Minister Modi need to stop fanning the flames of violence against non-hindus in India. Since the BJP government has been in power it has caused considerable tension in India amongst its different communities and in the region with its neighbours. Its desire of a 'hindutva' hindu nation and its pressure to try to 'hinduise its Christian, Muslim and other minorities' could cause an implosion within India and be a catalyst for a catastrophic war with its nuclear neighbour Pakistan. The fascist RSS group adheres to Nazi germany thinking, of which Prime minister Modi and his party are heavily influenced by (a lot of them have been members of the fascist group).

Ex-soldier & UN Peacekeeper, Raghu Raman, states the following, **"For all the chauvinistic war mongering touted in every medium, India cannot 'win' a war against Pakistan and the sooner we appreciate this politico-military reality, the more coherent and serious we will sound to our adversaries**

and the world community. The demands for a 'once and for all' resolution of Kashmir/Pakistan emanating from several quarters, which surprisingly includes some veterans – equating India's non-retaliation with impotence – perhaps don't factor the larger picture and the stark truth of modern military warfare". He further contends, **"Matter of fact, short of total genocide, no country regardless of its war-withal can hope to achieve a decisive victory with a 'short war' in today's world. As the US is discovering eight years, trillion dollars and over 25,000 casualties later - in Afghanistan. That era of 'decisive' short wars – especially in context of an Indo-Pak war is largely over because of several reasons".**[114]

India and Pakistan have to resolve the Kashmir issue amicably in order to avoid a never ending cycle of conflict. This conflict is having an adverse effect on the economies and the welfare of the people of South Asia.

Indian Soldiers on a border patrol

---

[114] Raghu Raman, Why war with Pakistan—is not an option -
https://medium.com/@captraman/why-war-with-pakistan-is-not-an-option-
3ccfa25a1529

Myanmar (Burma)

The Myanmar government of Aung San Suu Kyi's (with backing of its military) has been committing state terrorism against its Rohingya muslim minority population. There has been systematic killing, rape, torture and violations of human rights. Myanmar's armed forces and its police had started a major crackdown on its Rohingya people in Rakhine State. The attack by unidentified insurgents in October 2016 on Myanmar border post was the pretext used to attack its Rohingya population.

Rohingya Muslim 'genocide' committed by Myanmar's security forces

The United Nations have accused the Myanmar's government of ethnic cleansing and genocide. It had found widescale evidence of human rights violations, including extrajudicial killings, gang rapes, arson and infanticides. In addition, evidence of Myanmar's military and extremist Buddhists showed the increase persecution of the Rohingya population in 2017. Buddhist extremists started attacking the Rohingya people and committing atrocities against them. Evidence showed that the atrocities included attacks on Rohingya people and locations, looting and burning down Rohingya villages, mass killing of Rohingya civilians, gang rapes, and other sexual violence.[115]

---

[115] Myanmar's Military Planned Rohingya Genocide, Rights Group Says - https://www.nytimes.com/2018/07/19/world/asia/myanmar-rohingya-genocide.html

Aung San Suu Kyi with her senior generals

Médecins Sans Frontières (MSF) estimated in December 2017 that during the persecution, the military and the local Buddhists killed at least 10,000 Rohingya people. The military drive also displaced a large number of Rohingya people and made them refugees. According to the United Nations reports, as of January 2018, nearly 700,000 Rohingya people had fled or had been driven out of Rakhine state who then took shelter in the neighboring Bangladesh as refugees - after a campaign of mass slaughter, rape and village burnings in Rakhine State in Myanmar. There was evidence that this was the culmination of months of meticulous planning by the Myanmar security forces.[116]

---

[116] Ibid

Myanmar's military

Rohingya's forced into exile – their properties destroyed by Myanmar's military and extremist Buddhists.

Fortify Rights says that at least 27 Myanmar Army battalions, with up to 11,000 soldiers, and at least three combat police battalions, with around 900 personnel, participated in the bloodletting that began in late August and continued for weeks afterward.[117] Myanmar's military and civilian government have consistently described the crackdown as "clearance

---

[117] Myanmar authorities planned genocide against Rohingya, rights group claims - https://www.theguardian.com/global-development/2018/jul/19/myanmar-planned-genocide-against-rohingya-fortify-rights-claims-rakine-state

operations" against Muslim "terrorists."

Myanmar's military crackdown on the Rohingya's

Extremist Buddhists have killed many Rohingya's

However, US officials have said that, **"the violence amounted to a calculated campaign of ethnic cleansing, and one United Nations official described the anti-Rohingya campaign as bearing the hallmarks of genocide."** Aung San Suu Kyi's, the former nobel peace prize Laurette (1991) has not comdemned these killings and this has resulted in the revokation of the human rights award given by the United

States Holocaust Museum to her.[118] This was in view of her failure to use her 'moral authority' to halt a ruthless military campaign against its Rohingya minority population.[119]

Buddhists have been responsible for many of the killings of Rohingys's – they have been inciting many to kill.

---

[118] US Holocaust Museum withdraws Aung San Suu Kyi's human rights award - https://www.theguardian.com/world/2018/mar/07/aung-san-suu-kyi-holocaust-museum-award

[119] Myanmar's Military Planned Rohingya Genocide, Rights Group Says - https://www.nytimes.com/2018/07/19/world/asia/myanmar-rohingya-genocide.html

[119] Ibid

Aung San Suu Kyi defending her policies

Protests against the military crackdown on the Rohingya's

Rohingya's praying for safety from Myanmar's brutal 'genocidal' crackdown

Bosnia

In April 1992, the government of the Yugoslav republic of Bosnia-Herzegovina declared its independence from Yugoslavia. Over the next several years, Bosnian Serb forces, with the backing of the Serb-dominated Yugoslav army, perpetrated atrocious crimes against Bosniak (Bosnian Muslim) and Croatian civilians, resulting in the deaths of some 100,000 people (80 percent of them Bosniak) by 1995.[120] Over 2 million people were displaced and over 20,000 Bosniak Muslim women and girls raped. Some of the women were raped or sexually assaulted, while the men and boys who remained behind were killed immediately or bussed to mass killing sites. Estimates of Bosniaks killed by Serb forces at the UN protected Srebrenica range from around 7,000 to more than 8,000.[121]

---

[120] https://www.history.com/topics/bosnian-genocide

[121] https://www.history.com/topics/bosnian-genocide

The Serb forces ethnically cleansed the overwhelming majority of the non-Serb population at the command of Radovan Karadzic – head of the Serb Democratic Party (SDS), and the former Supreme Commander of the Bosnian Serb Army.[122] It was seen as the worst act of genocide since the Nazi regime's destruction of some 6 million European Jews during World War II

UN protected certain areas

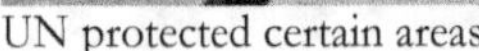

Civilians flee fighting in Vitez, Bosnia, in 1992[123]

Butchers of Bosnia - Radovan Karadzic (right) and his general Ratko Mladic pictured in April 1995.[124]

UN forces giving aid to those that are displaced by the conflict

---

[123] https://www.independent.co.uk/news/long_reads/bosnia-war-rape-survivors-speak-serbian-soldiers-balkans-women-justice-suffering-a7846546.html

[124] https://www.irishtimes.com/news/world/europe/bosnia-is-still-divided-ahead-of-radovan-karadzic-verdict-1.2584797

Family member at a grave of the mass killing by serbs forces on Bosniaks.

Bosnian prisoners

The atrocities faced by the people of Bosnia from the Serbs.

6 REASONS FOR TERRORISM

Neo Nazis and White Supremacists encircle and chant at counter protestors at the base of a statue of Thomas Jefferson after marching through the University of Virginia campus with torches in Charlottesville, Va., USA on August 11, 2017.[125]

Terrorists have resorted to various terror tactics, in order to achieve their goals, such as the following:

<u>Publicity</u>

Maybe the most basic aim of terrorism is to seize the attention of either the Governments or the population of the nation it targets, as terrorism expert Walter Laqueur points out:

"Terrorism has been with us for centuries, and it has always attracted inordinate attention because of its dramatic character and its sudden,

---

[125] Scott Gilmore on why we remain so focused on the bogeyman of Islamic terrorism when the most dangerous terror threat is far right extremism - https://www.macleans.ca/news/canada/the-rights-terrorism-problem/

often wholly unexpected, occurrence." [126]

Terrorism forces us to pay more attention to it whether we want to or not (primarily due to the concern for safety). This is normally a part of many terrorist attacks such as the Madrid Train bombings in 2004 (Spain), there was a lot of publicity for this event because of the large media coverage so many terrorist attack tactics have these similarities.[127]

Madrid train bombings

Another terrorist tactic to gain publicity is via Kidnapping and assassinating representatives of a state. For Instance, the Russian theatre siege in 2000, where Chechen rebels took control of a theatre in Moscow killing 160 and taking the rest as hostages. Russian Special Forces managed to kill the rebels using nerve gas but that also left 120 people dead. This incident gave the Chechen gunmen publicity to their cause of an independent Chechnya from Russia.[128]

---

[126] Walter Laqueur, The New Terrorism: Fanaticism and the Arms of Mass Destruction, Oxford, 1999.

[127] Madrid Train Bombings (Internet Website - Wikipedia, the free encyclopedia) http://en.wikipedia.org/wiki/Madrid_train_bombings

[128] Moscow theater hostage (Internet Website - Wikipedia, the free encyclopedia) http://en.wikipedia.org/wiki/Moscow_theater_hostage_crisis

Chechen gunmen seeking publicity to their cause via terrorism

Russian anti-terrorist troops in action

Russian Troops carrying out the rescue opertaion in the theatre

Communicating

Another reason for a terror tactic is to promote its message and the success of this is inextricably linked to the terrorist organisation itself. A well-organized group with distinct political aims is likely to be more successful in delivering its message than a disparate, non-focused organisation whose aim is to spread confusion and fear.[129]

ISIS using a number of terrorist methods for their cause

---

[129] (Alan Collins, Contemporary Security Studies, Oxford University Press, 2007, p293.

Shoko Asahara – leader of the doom cult Aum Shinrikyo

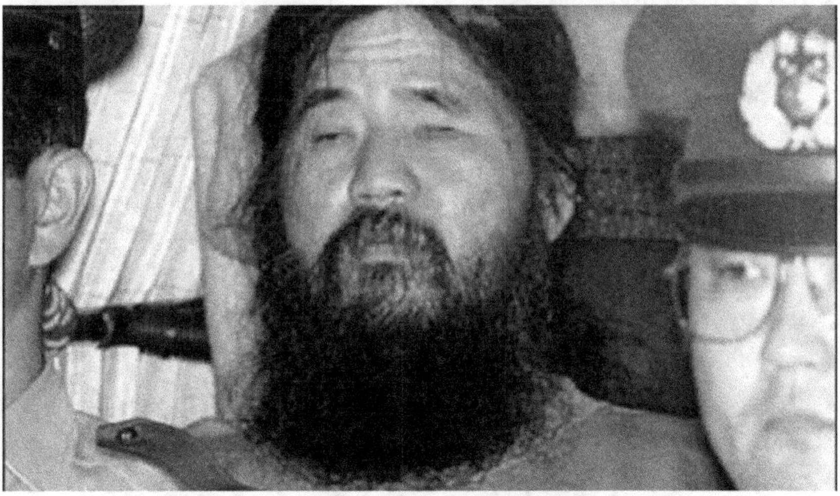

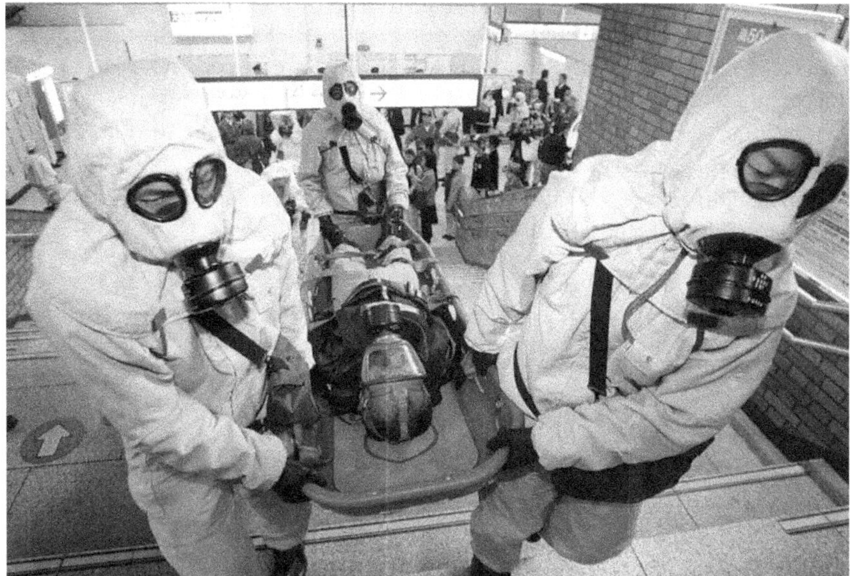

Deadly Tokyo subway sarin attack in 1995

In 1984 Shoko Asahara founded the Japanese doomsday cult - Aum Shinrikyo. It was responsible for the deadly Tokyo subway sarin attack in 1995 and was also responsible for another smaller sarin attack the previous year.

<u>Capability</u>

Another reason is to make small groups appear bigger than they really are. There are many groups around the world that use terror tactics to appear bigger than they really are. Recently in the news there are many suicide bomb attacks, car bomb and other attacks carried out in the Middle East by small groups. These tactics has made their particular group's look more powerful and has caused much fear amongst the people and thereby trying to make them give in to their demands.[130]

Eta Basque terrorist group in Spain have promised to renounce guns and bombs forever in its fight for an independent homeland[131]

---

[130] Ibid

[131] https://www.telegraph.co.uk/news/worldnews/europe/spain/7984567/Spains-government-rejects-Eta-ceasefire.html

Timothy McVeigh one of America's homegrown terrorist, had shocked the USA

The US homegrown terrorist timothy McVeigh killed 168 people by detonating a truck bomb in oklahoma City.

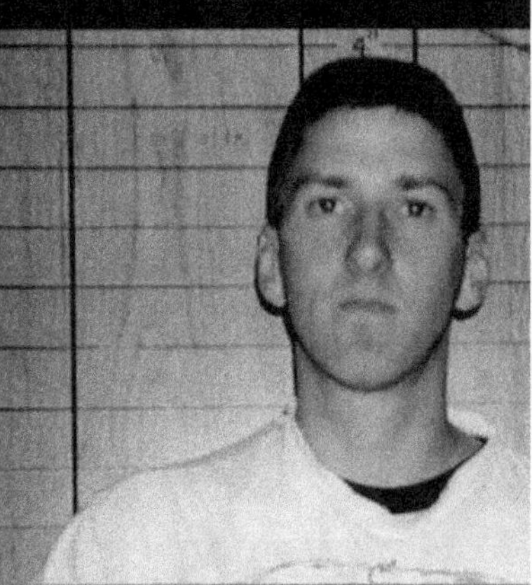

Message on a social media site in regards to terrorism and its perperators[132]

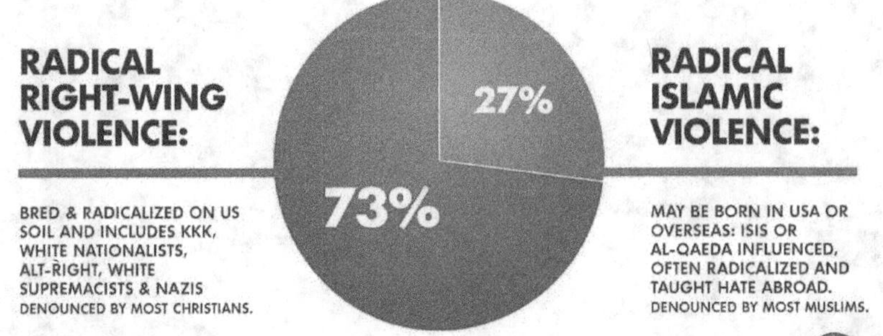

The Teror threat from the extremists of all walks of life [133]

---

[132] https://brickshistory.com/2017/03/09/timothy-mcveigh/

[133] http://wearethemedia.tv/opinion/2017/opinion-can-protect-free-speech-prosecute-right-wing-terrorists-time/

The FBI Admits Many Police Groups Are Now Infiltrated By The KKK (white supremacists)[134]

Anders Behring Breivik also known by his pseudonym Andrew Berwick, is a Norwegian far-right terrorist who committed the 2011 Norway attacks. On 22 July 2011 he killed eight people by detonating a van bomb amid Regjeringskvartalet in Oslo, then shot dead 69 participants of a Workers'

[134] http://wearethemedia.tv/opinion/2017/opinion-can-protect-free-speech-prosecute-right-wing-terrorists-time/

Youth League (AUF) summer camp on the island of Utoya. In August 2012 he was convicted of mass murder, causing a fatal explosion, and terrorism.[135]

Anders Behring Breivik makes a far right salute as he enters court on April 16, 2012, the first day of his trial.

Social Media – alternative narrative: Muslims are not terrorist as the media portrays (primarily in western media)[136]

---

[135] Anders Behring Breivik And The Deadliest Mass Shooting In Recorded History - https://allthatsinteresting.com/anders-behring-breivik

[136] Muslims Are Not Terrorists: A Factual Look at Terrorism and Islam - https://www.huffingtonpost.com/omar-alnatour/muslims-are-not-

Undermining Morale

Indiscriminate bombing has been used with the aim of undermining the will and morale of a community. An example of a group that used this tactic was the IRA which fought against British rule of Northern Ireland. One particular incident was the IRA attack in 1996 of London (Dockland Bombings). They continued bombing and killing innocent civilians to achieve the political goal of a united Ireland. Doing this could make a government give in to demands and stop the bombings.[137] Other attacks have these similarities such as the regular suicide bombings in the Middle East from groups such as 'Hamas' or 'Hezbollah' against Israel. There have also been car bomb attacks in Iraq against the US troops in order to make it more difficult for the US to operate and eventually force them to leave the country.[138]

Hamas soldiers

---

terrorist_b_8718000.html
[137] Docklands Bombing (Internet Website - Wikipedia, the free encyclopedia) http://en.wikipedia.org/wiki/1996_Docklands_bombing
[138] Terrorist incidents (Internet Website - Wikipedia, the free encyclopedia) http://en.wikipedia.org/wiki/List_of_terrorist_incidents

Aftermath of the IRA London Docklands bombing

Hezbollah parade

Another example is that of Afghanistan, where many bomb attacks are used to destabilise the country. The reason they do this, is that they do not support the government as it has close relations with the US which invaded the country in 2001 to topple the Taliban government. Using bomb attacks will undermine the people's confidence in their government because they are not doing a good enough job of stopping the bombings.[139]

<u>Provocation</u>

Terrorism has been used in the hope of increasing government repression, or an overreaction or retaliation. The tactic is to provoke a reaction that will alienate the population from the government. For example, the 9/11 attacks on America had provoked the American government to start their 'War on Terrorism'. This aimed to stop terrorism in the world and destroy or capture groups like Al-Qaeda. Another example is the Tiananmen Square protests in China, the protestors did not use terrorism but they did make the government use terrorism which alienated the government from its people.[140]

Stirring up emotions?

As can be seen from the above, to explain terrorism is not an easy task. There are many definitions explaining terrorism but the question is, which one fits your needs and thoughts? Through the publicity generated by their

---

[139] Ibid

[140] Earl Conteh-Morgan, Collective Political Violence – An Introduction to the Theories and Cases of Violent Conflicts, Routledge, 2004, p259.

violence, terrorist seek to obtain the leverage, influence and power they otherwise lack to effect political change on either a national or international scale.[141]

Groups can be labelled 'terrorists' at the will of governments, but not all 'terrorist groups are terrorist. Such labelling is a convenient way of stigmatizing what under other conditions would be a legitimate opposition to a regime, its leadership, or its policies.

According to White,

"The definition of terrorism depends on political power. Governments can increase their power when they label opponents as 'terrorists.' Citizens seem willing to accept more abuses of governmental power when a counterterrorist campaign is in progress, 'Terrorists' do not enjoy the same humanitarian privileges as 'people.' In the public mind, illegal arrest and sometimes even torture and murder are acceptable methods of dealing with terrorists. Labelling can have deadly results".[142]

As can be seen, there can be state-sponsored terrorism as well as group-driven terrorist networks.

Professor Eqbal Ahmad sees the definition of terrorism as not being examined enough. Ahmad sees all these definitions of terrorism as a way of stirring up emotions in the mind of the people. Ahmad points out that most people don't look at the reasons why people resort to terrorism. He believes that one must understand why there is terrorism before one can learn how to stop it. He also states that most people don't take into consideration how emotions play a large role on how terrorism starts.[143]

---

[141] Ibid
[142142] William Crotty, Democratic development and Political Terrorism – The Global Perspective, Northeastern University Press, 2005, p8.
[143] Terrorism theirs and ours (Internet Website) – by Eqbal Ahmed
http://www.sangam.org/ANALYSIS/Ahmad.htm

7 KILLED MORE THAN 20 MILLION PEOPLE

The US currently being the sole Superpower has caused the death of over 20 million people since World War II according to a number of studies.[144] It has under the pretext of various reasons, invaded and caused instability in many countries across the world. It is currently said that the US drops a bomb somewhere in the world every 12 minutes – this indicates the sheer scale of bombardment it has undertaken.[145] US munitions factory are currently unable to compete with the demand that the US military has put – despite spending $20 billion more on munitions.

This can be argued to show, 'State Terrorism' at its best – the US is a master in this field. Every time it drops a bomb, there will be many

---

[144] James Lucas (2015). US Has Killed More Than 20 Million People in 37 "Victim Nations" Since World War II - https://www.globalresearch.ca/us-has-killed-more-than-20-million-people-in-37-victim-nations-since-world-war-ii/5492051

[145] Every 12 Minutes, the United States Drops a Bomb Somewhere - https://www.thenewamerican.com/usnews/foreign-policy/item/29382-every-12-minutes-the-united-states-drops-a-bomb-somewhere

casualties – usually the innocent civilian population. The US has been the main cause of interferences in many nations and have used coercive, bullying and intimidating tactics to subdue any nation that does not agree with it. It gives a message of peaceful intentions and states that it offers the best way of life – but in reality to the vast majority of the world it has become the opposite. It has either directly attacked another country or have instigated proxy forces to fight a battle on its behalf.

US soldiers on a patrol

The study indicates that the US was directly responsible for conflicts such as the Korean war and the Vietnam war – causing between 10-15 million deaths (including those of the Chinese in Korea and Cambodia and Laos in Vietnam war).[146]

In addition, there were between 9 and 14 million killings by the US (direct and proxy wars) in Afghanistan, Angola, Democratic Republic of the Congo, East Timor, Guatemala, Indonesia, Pakistan and Sudan.[147]

---

[146] James Lucas (2015). US Has Killed More Than 20 Million People in 37 "Victim Nations" Since World War II - https://www.globalresearch.ca/us-has-killed-more-than-20-million-people-in-37-victim-nations-since-world-war-ii/5492051

[147] James Lucas (2015). US Has Killed More Than 20 Million People in 37 "Victim Nations" Since World War II - https://www.globalresearch.ca/us-has-killed-more-than-20-million-people-in-37-victim-nations-since-world-war-ii/5492051

The study indicates that across the world an estimated of 20-30 million have been killed via the action of the Americans.

In view of the above killings, James Lucas stated, **"To the families and friends of these victims it makes little difference whether the causes were U.S. military action, proxy military forces, the provision of U.S. military supplies or advisors, or other ways, such as economic pressures applied by our nation. They had to make decisions about other things such as finding lost loved ones, whether to become refugees, and how to survive"**.

And further says, **"And the pain and anger is spread even further. Some authorities estimate that there are as many as 10 wounded for each person who dies in wars. Their visible, continued suffering is a continuing reminder to their fellow countrymen"**. He further poses the question, **"How many September 11ths has the United States caused in other nations since WWII?" The answer is: possibly 10,000"**.[148]

We will look briefly at some of the atrocities committed directly or by proxy US forces.

---

[148] Ibid

Every 12 Minutes, the United States Drops a Bomb Somewhere[149]

The above atrocities committed by the US are well documented in many reference books. Conflicts such as the Vietnam wars, Iraq, Afghanistan etc., show clearly the suffering suffered by the populations in these countries.

US intervention in the Vietnam caused much destruction and loss of life in Vietnam and surrounding nations. Killings like the Mai Lai massacre had shocked the world. My Lai massacre: the day US troops slaughtered 504 unarmed Vietnamese civilians in three brutal hours.

---

[149] Every 12 Minutes, the United States Drops a Bomb Somewhere - https://www.thenewamerican.com/usnews/foreign-policy/item/29382-every-12-minutes-the-united-states-drops-a-bomb-somewhere

On March 16, 1968, hundreds of civilians were killed by American soldiers. [150]

[150] https://www.scmp.com/news/asia/southeast-asia/article/2137372/my-lai-massacre-day-us-troops-slaughtered-504-unarmed

More than 500 defenceless Vietnamese people were slaughtered by the US military in the My Lai massacre.[151]

The My Lai massacre took place when 115 US troops (Charlie Company, 1st Battalion, 20th Infantry) landed in helicopters just outside the village. Within four hours US soldiers (including their military high command, who were flying overhead in helicopters) were participating and observing in the civilian massacre.[152]

Iraq

The war in Iraq has shown the massive loss of lives – a country totally destroyed in the pretext of weapons of mass destruction (WMD), which after the destruction of the country were confirmed at not having any. Millions of Iraqi military and civilian populations suffered from sanctions, torture, widespread killings by US forces. The Iraqi people were subjected to psychological warfare and were humiliated and killed in great numbers.

---

[151] Fifty years after the US military's My Lai massacre -
https://www.greenleft.org.au/content/fifty-years-after-us-militarys-my-lai-massacre-gi-resistance-continues-videos

[152] My Lai massacre (Vietnam): 49 years later - http://global-politics.eu/lai-massacre-vietnam-49-years-later/

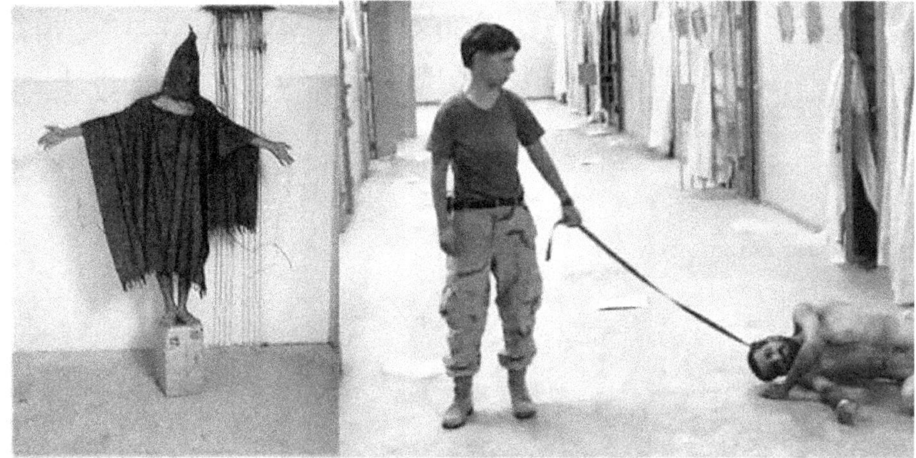

US troops torturing and terrorisng Iraqi civilians

Afghanistan

The 'Kill Team' Images that further shocked the world

A group of US soldiers have murdered innocent civilians and then taken a 'trophy' pictures with the dead body. Many Afghanistan's were killed this way. There were further pictures of US troops defiling (urinating on Afghan dead). The question asks, that how many other regions have US troops got away with this kind of sadistic behaviour and murder. SPIEGEL published some of the photos -- and the US military responded promptly with an apology. [153]

Guantanamo bay

US soldiers particpating in a culture of torture and terrorism

---

[153] US Army Apologizes for Horrific Photos from Afghanistan - http://www.spiegel.de/international/world/the-kill-team-images-us-army-apologizes-for-horrific-photos-from-afghanistan-a-752310.html

http://archivo.elcomercio.pe/mundo/actualidad/liberaron-al-lider-abusos-prision-iraqui-abu-ghraib-noticia-984571

Torture undertaken by US soldiers – authorised indirectly by US leadership (a justification of state terrorism methods).

The above are just some examples, the pattern could be found I many countries, Such as Syria. In order to support this global killing machine, shocking amount money has been spent on this. The War on Terror that was launched by the Bush administration in light of the 911 terrorist attacks has resulted in massive costs. According to the analyst, Kimberly Amadeo, "The War on Terror includes the Afghanistan War and the War in Iraq. It added $2 trillion to the debt as of the FY 2018 budget".[154]

War on Terror Costs Summary Table (in billions)

FY	WoT OCO	DoD Budget Increase	VA Budget Increase	Total WoT	Boots on Ground*

---

[154] Kimberly Amadeo (2018). War on Terror Facts, Costs, and Timeline - Whose Spent More on War? Bush, Obama, or Trump? https://www.thebalance.com/war-on-terror-facts-costs-timeline-3306300

Year					
2001	$22.9	$6.5	$1.5	$31.0	9,700
2002	$16.9	$40.8	$1.5	$59.1	9,700
2003	$72.5	$36.7	$2.6	$111.9	136,800
2004	$90.8	$11.6	$2.6	$105.0	169,900
2005	$75.6	$23.6	$3.1	$102.3	175,803
2006	$115.8	$10.5	$0.7	$127.0	154,220
2007	$166.3	$20.9	$5.3	$192.5	186,563
2008	$186.9	$47.5	$1.2	$235.6	181,000
2009	$153.1	$34.2	$9.8	$197.1	183,300
2010	$162.4	$14.7	$3.9	$181.0	144,205
2011	$158.8	$0.3	$3.3	$162.4	105,555
2012	$115.1	$2.2	$2.3	$119.6	65,800
2013	$82.0	-$34.9	$2.6	$49.6	43,300
2014	$85.2	$0.8	$2.0	$88.0	32,500
2015	$64.2	$1.0	$1.8	$67.0	12,650
2016	$58.6	$24.3	$6.5	$89.5	12,457
2017	$82.4	-$5.6	$3.5	$80.3	n.a.
2018	$64.6	$58.4	$3.8	$126.8	n.a.
TOTAL	**$1,774.1**	**$293.6**	**$58.0**	**$2,125.7**	

(Source: "National Defense Budget Estimates for FY 2018," Office of the Under Secretary of Defense, June 2017.)[155]

The effect on the US economy has been an extra $2.1 trillion in debt added as a cause of the War on Terror.[156] The War in Iraq killed 4,488 U.S.

---

[155] Kimberly Amadeo (2018). War on Terror Facts, Costs, and Timeline - Whose Spent More on War? Bush, Obama, or Trump? https://www.thebalance.com/war-on-terror-facts-costs-timeline-3306300

[156] https://www.thebalance.com/war-on-terror-facts-costs-timeline-3306300

soldiers and wounded 32,226 more. US Taxpayers spent more than $800 billion on the Iraq War alone. [157]

The increase defence spending had led to a huge US debt crisis - that's $19 trillion total debt. [158]

America at war

The US has been in conflict with many nations and the list below will show an indication of the level of attacks since World War II (there are more countries to add, but this should give a rough idea of the countries that have been attacked by the US).[159]

---

[157] Kimberly Amadeo (2018). How the 9/11 Attacks Affect the Economy Today - https://www.thebalance.com/how-the-9-11-attacks-still-affect-the-economy-today-3305536

[158] https://www.thebalance.com/how-the-9-11-attacks-still-affect-the-economy-today-3305536

[159] William Blum (2018). United States Bombings of Other Countries. America's "Bombing List" - https://www.globalresearch.ca/united-states-bombings-of-other-countries-americas-bombing-list/5533371

The bombing list[160]

1. Korea and China 1950-53 (Korean War)
2. Guatemala 1954
3. Indonesia 1958
4. Cuba 1959-1961
5. Guatemala 1960
6. Congo 1964

---

[160] William Blum (2018). United States Bombings of Other Countries. America's "Bombing List" - https://www.globalresearch.ca/united-states-bombings-of-other-countries-americas-bombing-list/5533371

7. Laos 1964-73
8. Vietnam 1961-73
9. Cambodia 1969-70
10. Guatemala 1967-69
11. Grenada 1983
12. Lebanon 1983, 1984 (both Lebanese and Syrian targets)
13. Libya 1986
14. El Salvador 1980s
15. Nicaragua 1980s
16. Iran 1987
17. Panama 1989
18. Iraq 1991 (Persian Gulf War)
19. Kuwait 1991
20. Somalia 1993
21. Bosnia 1994, 1995
22. Sudan 1998
23. Afghanistan 1998
24. Yugoslavia 1999
25. Yemen 2002
26. Iraq 1991-2003 (US/UK on regular basis)
27. Iraq 2003-2015
28. Afghanistan 2001-2015
29. Pakistan 2007-2015
30. Somalia 2007-8, 2011
31. Yemen 2009, 2011
32. Libya 2011, 2015
33. Syria 2014-2015

Plus many others.

The publisher of a nonviolence website, Martin Kelly said, **"We never see the smoke and the fire, we never smell the blood, we never see the terror in the eyes of the children, whose nightmares will now feature screaming missiles from unseen terrorists, known only as Americans".**[161]

---

[161]   https://www.globalresearch.ca/united-states-bombings-of-other-countries-americas-bombing-list/5533371

https://vagamundos.com/reflexiones-de-un-vagamundos-sobre-la-posguerra/

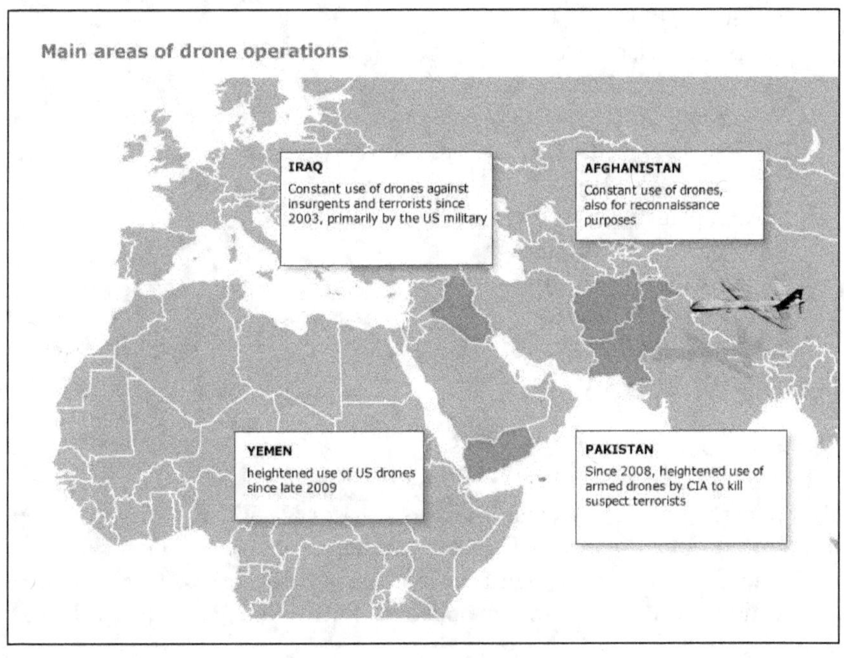

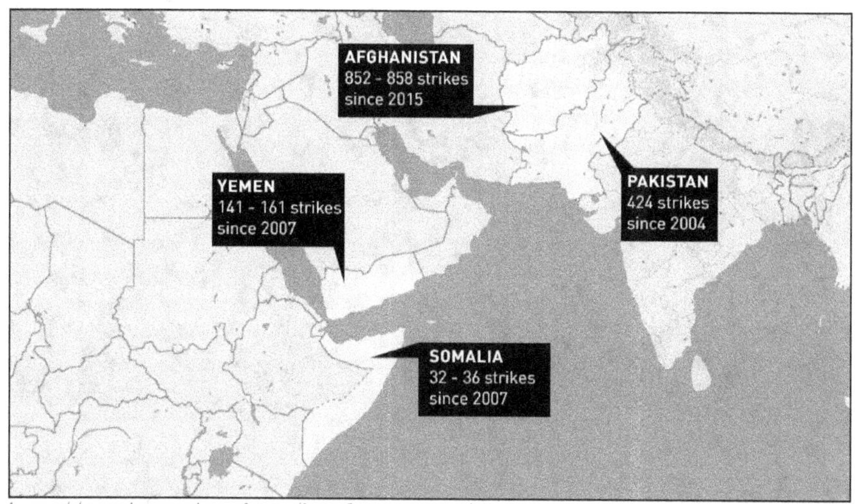

https://newsinteractives.cbc.ca/longform-custom/american-dreamer-barack-obama-foreign-policy-legacy

Drone UCAV

US troops in Afghanistan

US troops on a mission

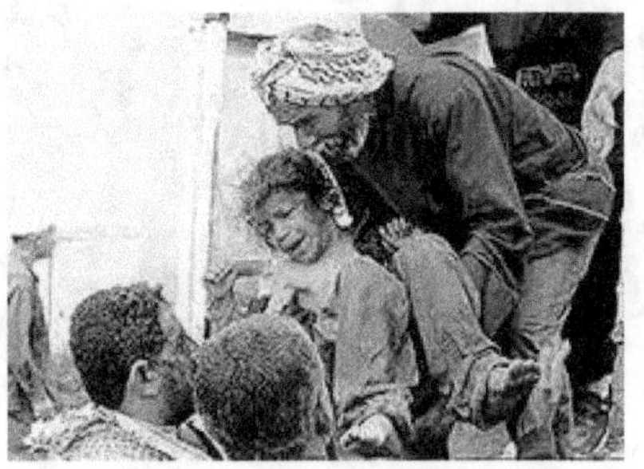

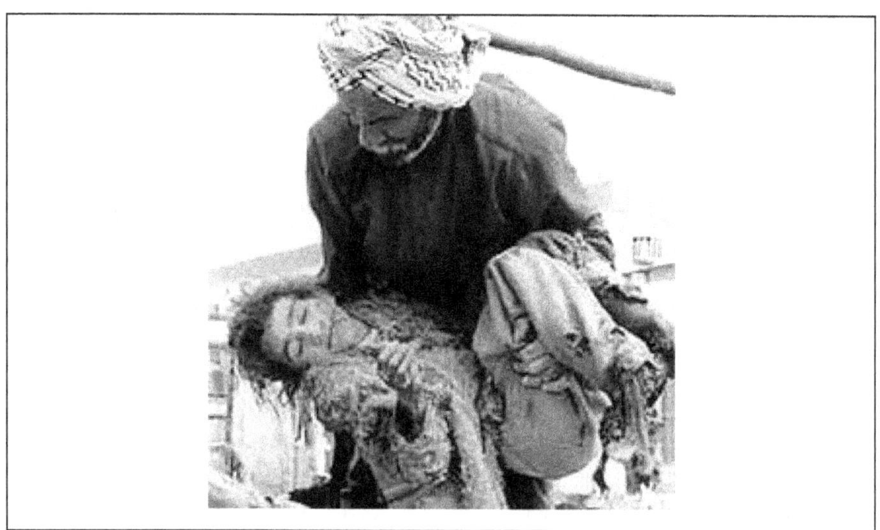

This is the reality of the war (these are the consequences)[162]

A 2014 Gallup poll taken among 66,000 people in 65 nations revealed the USA is considered to be the greatest threat to peace. (HUFFINGTON POST – 2014) [163]

The US and its people see themselves as a peace-loving nations, but the evidence is in contrary to this. It shows that the Americans are addicted to War and its version of democracy is flawed and dangerous as it always attempts to destroy countries under the pretext of regime changes etc.[164]

Terrorism - Western wars have killed four million Muslims since 1990

Western wars have killed four million Muslims since 1990.[165] This number has been obtained from the study conducted by the reputable Washington DC-based Physicians for Social Responsibility (PRS). The PSR study is

---

[162] https://vagamundos.com/reflexiones-de-un-vagamundos-sobre-la-posguerra/

[163] https://www.popularresistance.org/us-has-killed-more-than-20-million-in-37-nations-since-wwii/

[164] Ibid

[165] Nafeez Ahmed (2015). war, USA, Humanitarian Crisis, IDP's, Refugees http://www.middleeasteye.net/columns/unworthy-victims-western-wars-have-killed-four-million-muslims-1990-39149394

authored health experts, including Dr Robert Gould of the University of California San Francisco Medical centre and Professor Tim Takaro of Simon Fraser University. PRS comprises of Nobel-Peace Prize-winning doctors group and had concluded that the 'War on Terror' in a span of 10 years since 9/11 attacks had killed between 1.3 million – 2 million people.

The study was a 97 page report that is described by The former UN assistant secretary-general Dr Hans von Sponeck has described the 97 page report by PRS, as **"a significant contribution to narrowing the gap between reliable estimates of victims of war, especially civilians in Iraq, Afghanistan and Pakistan and tendentious, manipulated or even fraudulent accounts".[166]**

The PRS report looks primarily at the civilian casualties from the US led interventions in Iraq, Afghanistan and Pakistan. The Lancet study that estimated 655,000 Iraq deaths up to 2006 (and over a million until today by extrapolation) was considered fairly accurate by the PRS report. Furthermore, the PSR study adds at least 220,000 in Afghanistan and 80,000 in Pakistan that have been killed as the direct or indirect consequence of US-led war: A figure between 1.3 – 2 million has been given.[167]

US troops

---

[166] Ibid

[167] Nafeez Ahmed (2015). war, USA, Humanitarian Crisis, IDP's, Refugees http://www.middleeasteye.net/columns/unworthy-victims-western-wars-have-killed-four-million-muslims-1990-39149394

http://www.voltairenet.org/article187299.html

Iraq

The war on Iraq began in 1991 with the first Gulf War and was followed by the UN sanctions regime. Undisputed UN figures show that 1.7 million Iraqi civilians died due to the West's brutal sanctions regime, half of whom were children. It is estimated that the US led war from 1991 – 2003 killed 1.9 million Iraqis. A further 1 million people were killed from 2003 onwards – making a total of 2.9 million civilian deaths alone in Iraq.[168]

---

[168] Ibid

'In Iraq alone, the US-led war from 1991 to 2003 killed 1.9 million Iraqis'[169]

Afghanistan

It is estimated that in Afghanistan the killings of civilians could be between 3-5 million, due to the US led intervention in the region.[170]

The investigative journalist and international security expert, Dr Nafeez Ahmed, states, **"Western interventions in Iraq and Afghanistan since the 1990s - from direct killings and the longer-term impact of war-imposed deprivation - likely constitute around 4 million (2 million in Iraq from 1991-2003, plus 2 million from the "war on terror"), and could be as high as 6-8 million people when accounting for higher avoidable death estimates in Afghanistan".**[171]

He further states, **"Much of this death has been justified in the context of fighting tyranny and terrorism. Yet thanks to the silence of the wider media, most people have no idea of the true scale of protracted terror wrought in their name by US and UK tyranny in Iraq and Afghanistan".**[172]

---

[169] Nafeez Ahmed (2017). Unworthy Victims: Western Wars Have Killed Four Million Muslims Since 1990 -
http://www.stopwar.org.uk/index.php/news-comment/2615-unworthy-victims-western-wars-have-killed-four-million-muslims-since-1990

[170] Ibid

[171] Unworthy victims – Western Wars have killed four million Muslims:
http://www.middleeasteye.net/columns/unworthy-victims-western-wars-have-killed-four-million-muslims-1990-39149394

[172] Unworthy victims – Western Wars have killed four million Muslims:
http://www.middleeasteye.net/columns/unworthy-victims-western-wars-have-killed-four-

The writers Waldman and Hugh Pope of the Wall Street Journal stated (in reference George W Bush's statement on the 9/11 attacks):

"President Bush vowed ... to 'rid the world of evil-doers,' then cautioned: 'This crusade, this war on terrorism, is going to take a while.'

Crusade? In strict usage, the word describes the Christian military expeditions a millennium ago to capture the Holy Land from Muslims. But in much of the Islamic world, where history and religion suffuse daily life in ways unfathomable to most Americans, it is shorthand for something else: a cultural and economic Western invasion that, Muslims fear, could subjugate them and desecrate Islam".[173]

The US led 'War on Terror' has gradually destroyed the infrastructure of these countries and also killing millions of Muslims – some would say it is a kind of murder frenzy committed by the US and its participants into this conflict. It can be argued that these are war crimes and indication of genocide committed by these rogue individuals that are in power, albeit either in the USA or other western governments. Accountability of these 'criminals' need to be made in order to avoid future mass slaughter and a never ending cycle of terrorism – whether it is state terrorism or not.[174]

Polls: US Is 'the Greatest Threat to Peace in the World Today'

Biggest Threat to World

million-muslims-1990-39149394

[173] Kit O'Connell (2016). Four Million Muslims Killed In Western Wars: Should We Call It Genocide? https://www.globalresearch.ca/four-million-muslims-killed-in-western-wars-should-we-call-it-genocide/5541926

[174] Kit O'Connell (2016). Four Million Muslims Killed In Western Wars: Should We Call It Genocide? https://www.globalresearch.ca/four-million-muslims-killed-in-western-wars-should-we-call-it-genocide/5541926

Peace: The United States

International polls shows that world, including significant portion of Americans, deem US as greatest obstacle to peace

https://www.commondreams.org/news/2013/12/31/biggest-threat-world-peace-united-states

https://www.strategic-culture.org/news/2017/08/07/polls-us-greatest-threat-to-peace-world-today.html

US led coalition bombs Syria

8 PEACE EDUCATION

The modern world has been prone to an increasing trend in destructive conflicts and wars that have devastated regions across the globe. Since the  First World War, there has been a rapid increase in the development of various methods to kill one another. The massive loss of lives and the human suffering (and also environmental degradation) has continued with an increase in lethality and fervour. Harris (2004) states, "During this past century there has been growth in social concerns about horrific forms of violence, like ecocide, genocide, modern warfare, ethnic hatred, racism, sexual abuse and domestic violence".

Many countries are currently been shaken by violent and intractable conflicts, including Iraq, Syria, Israel, Nigeria, Ukraine and Yemen. The list continues with a number of conflicts across the world that have the potential to cause huge loss of life. The conflict over the disputed territory of Kashmir between India and Pakistan has the potential to escalate to a nuclear level (as both countries possess nuclear weapons).

Harris (2004) further mentions that there is, "a corresponding growth in the field of peace education where educators, from early child care to adult, use their professional skills to warn fellow citizens about imminent dangers and advise them about paths to peace".

Culp (2017) argues that, "in the context of violent and intractable conflicts, peace education appears to be an effective instrument to promote peace because it holds the promise to empower future generations to solve many of those problems which present generations have had difficulty resolving". Culp further contends (2017), "Teaching people to interact with each other on peaceful terms is vital for social life of all groups – and even in the absence of any crisis".

Peace Studies does not have a clear agreed definition at this moment. Butt et al., (2011), noted, "Peace is a vague word. For some it means silence, calm and quiet, while other perceive it is an "end to quarrel", no conflict, no war, no violence, or no dispute (Mehmooda, 2006). According to Harris and Synott, Peace Education is a successions of 'teaching encounters' that

draw from people:
1)   People's want for peace,
2)   Non-violent alternatives for dealing with conflict
3)   Skills for critical examination of structural measures that produce and legitimize injustice and equality (Harris and Synott, 2004).

Danesh (2006) argues that peace education is an elusive concept and has become more important due to the ever increasing trend of conflicts across the world. Accordingly, current peace education activities have been put under four categories:

Peace education 'mainly as a matter of changing mind-set', peace education 'mainly as a matter of cultivating a set of skills', peace education 'mainly a matter of promoting human rights, and finally, peace education as a 'matter of environmentalism, disarmament, and the promotion of a culture of peace' (Salomon, 2002). Moreover, ten goals for effective peace education had been identified by Harris (2002).

This shows that there has been widespread debate amongst the international community in regards to finding ways of increasing human security via the various processes of peace education.

Ellison (2014), noted the important study by Bush and Satarelli (2000) that had highlighted the "two faces of education and its role in both fuelling and mitigating conflict". In this study a number of examples were provided to show the ways in which education was used to intensify intergroup hostility. Such as the following:

(1) Education used as a weapon in cultural repression (the refusal to allow the Kurdish minority in Turkey to use their language in schools),
(2) Denial of education as a weapon of war (destruction of schools in Mozambique and the forced closure of Palestinian schools by Israel),
(3) Manipulation of textbooks (negative ethnic stereotypes in Rwanda and depiction of Tamils as the historic enemies of the Sinhalese in Sri Lanka).

Ellison (2014) also mentions the numerous studies that have discussed the many ways that the school system might reproduce social and gender inequalities that may be a catalyst for war (Davis, 2004).

Butt et al., (2011), noted, "Peace education is educating all people for peace to satisfy their physical and social needs through individual and group action at the micro (interpersonal) and macro (local, national, and global inter group) levels" (Yousaf et al., 2010). In addition, "The aim of peace education is to draw out, enrich, deepen and place in context students' thinking about the concept of peace" (Bretherton, et al., 2002)

The globalisation of the world and the regular tourism across it has led some to expand on the concept of peace. Ward (2009) has used the term 'peace tourism' in which he describes the term as, "self-initiated travel by an individual citizen to explore a (new) nation and its people using personal resources – time, financial, interpersonal, etc.". He believes that this concept is relevant to, "citizens of nations involved in war, genocide, drug or human trafficking, arms sales or any systematic armed violence against other nations".

Butt et al., (2011), also mentions "that internet, cd-rom, children's books, traditional folk stories, proverbs, art work and artefacts, and language teaching can be used as creative avenues to introduce peace education concepts, skills and attitudes, whether in or out of the school context" (Fountain, Susan, 1999).

The daily news of violent conflicts around the world and the trade in the buying and selling of weapons has increased human misery, poverty and loss of life. Peace education is a way of embedding positive methods to reduce the arms trade and ensure a more peaceful world.

Peace Education needs to become mandatory in all educational institutions and also should be a requirement for all government employees - confirms the positivity in this area and the desire to have this implemented in general education. Butt et al., (2011), further contends, "Peace education is most effective when the skills of peace and conflict resolution are learned actively and are modelled by the school environment in which pupils are taught" (Baldo and Furniss, 1998).

Peace Education can reform individuals positively. Butt et al., (2011), stated "Peace Education is currently considered to be both a philosophy and a process involving skill, including listening, reflection, problem solving, co-operation and conflict resolution. The process involves empowering people with the skills, attitude and knowledge to create a safe world and build a sustainable environment. The philosophy teaches nonviolence, love, compassion, and reverence for all life" (Harris and Morrison, 1988).

There is a high chance that peace education can reduce the issues such as terrorism, arms trade, proliferation of WMD etc. If more and more people are aware of the alternative methods of resolving conflicts and with individual mind-set changed positively towards a peaceful world. – then the scourge of the global arms trade and terrorism can be curtailed. The arms trade is the mechanism that fuels the simmering disputes and conflicts across the world.

People across the world need to understand the root causes of terrorism and its various forms. Societies such as the USA need to look into, why most of the world persieve them as a threat (global polls). The gun culture (cowboy type) and its fascination with killing needs to be addressed. It is argued that currently it is the most effective terrorist machine (state terrorism at its best).

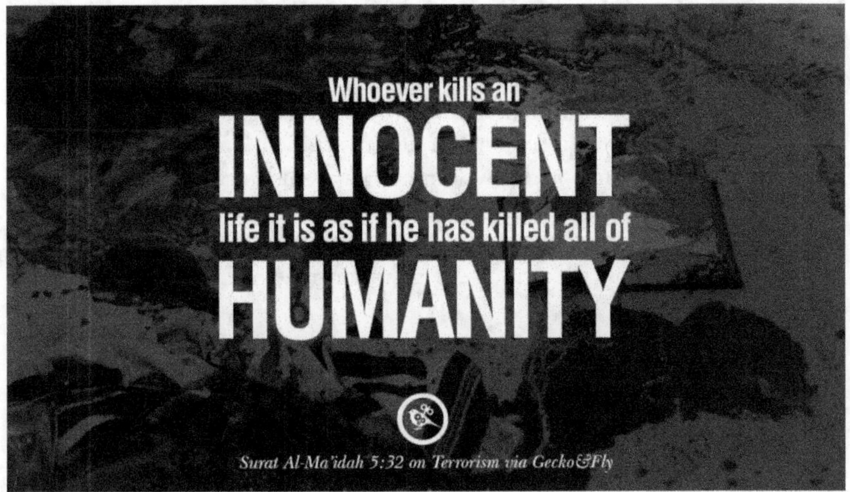

Surat Al-Ma'idah 5:32 on Terrorism via Gecko&Fly

9 CONCLUSION

US soldier Mike Prysner - http://19.org/blog/real-terrorist/

Any discussion of terrorism has to firstly define its terms: what do we mean by terrorism and how does it manifest itself in contemporary accounts and moreover, what is the difference between legitimate military action and one based on terror? The definitions of terrorism are complex and depend, to a very large extent, on who one is asking. A Government defence adviser would, for instance, have a markedly different notion of what constitutes terrorism than a member of a paramilitary organisation and an ordinary member of the public might have a notion based somewhere on the interaction between these two depending on their socio-cultural background.

For Instance, in the Middle East, or Spain or Northern Ireland, it would be possible, we could imagine, for definitions of terrorism to vary from area to area and from street to street depending on political and cultural allegiances. As stated by Peter Sederberg:

"The relative absence of a consensus on meaning leads to an indefinite number of competing ideas of terrorism. Indeed, a recent catalogue identifies over a hundred definitions. Moreover, we cannot conclude that these various definitions merely represent different

ways of saying the same thing." [175]

Governments, such as the American and UK administrations, have tended to stress the notion of terrorism as being based on its non-combatants victims and the extent that it represents the 'calculated use of threat of violence to inculcate fear, intended to coerce or intimidate governments or societies'. Such definitions, although useful in genuine debate, are of little use when it comes to discerning exactly what terrorist activity is, much of modern state warfare consist of exactly the same activity: the spreading of fear and intimidation through governments and populations and yet would seldom be classed as acts of terrorism. The notion of terrorism, in the contemporary political media has generally come to mean any practice that is considered wrong or counter to the practices and policies of its target.[176]

Arguments for the lack of a universal definition are as follows. Almost every serious attempt to define the term have been sponsored by governments who instinctively attempt to draw a definition which <u>excludes</u> bodies like themselves. Any definition that could be agreed upon in, say, Western countries would be biased towards those in non-western countries.[177]

Virtually no organisation openly calls itself terrorist, on the contrary, many groups call all their enemies 'terrorist'. The word is very loosely applied and very difficult to challenge when it is being used inappropriately, for example in war situations or against non-violent persons. There are many numerous occassions when violence by established governments is sold as 'defence', even when that claim is considered dubious by some; any attempt to oppose the established order through military means, however, is often labelled 'terrorism'.[178]

If we labelled groups 'terrorist' on the basis of how their opponents perceive them, such labels would be very controversial, for example: State of Israel, USA, Syria, Iraq, Iran, Afghanistan etc under the perception of groups such as the Taleban. Groups conducting revolution, such as the Communist Party of Nepal (Maoist), are routinely denigrated as 'terrorist' Almost all guerrilla groups (like Tamil Tigers or Chechen rebels) are accused of being 'terrorist', but almost all guerrilla groups accuse countries

---

[175] Peter Sederberg, Terrorist: Myths, Illusion, Rhetoric and Reality, London; Prentice Hall, 1989.

[176] Ibid

[177] Terrorism (Internet Website - Wikipedia, the free encyclopedia) www. http://en.wikipedia.org/wiki/Terrorism, 2007.

[178] Peter Hough, Understanding Global Security, pg62, Routledge, 2004.

they fight against of likewise being 'terrorist'. Moreover, the term could also include the many resistance movements during World War II.

All in all, terrorism is hard to define. The question of defining terrorism is that it is very hard to be differentiated from acts of war, 'just' or 'unjust'. Some would consider War and Terrorism as the same, since the death of innocent civilians is the aftermath of either of them.

As indicated above, there are many reasons why political groups attempt to bring about radical change through terrorism. People are often frustrated with their position in society. They may in some way feel persecuted or oppressed because of their race, religion, or they feel exploited by a government. Any group that uses terrorist actions have very complex and powerful reasons to engage in those activities.

The usual experience of violence by a stronger party has historically turned victims into terrorists. State terror very often breeds collective terror. Because 'terrorism' is a word that has been used so much and so loosely that it has lost a clear meaning. The main problem that arises is that terrorism is used to define force, based on whether the author agrees with the goals of the violence.

Overall, as can be seen, terrorism can come in many different forms but there will always be debate on whether something really can be classed as terrorism or not. This can be summed up in the saying, **"one man's terrorist is another man's freedom fighter"**. (41) It is unlikely that we will ever see an end to terrorism. It can be argued that terrorists are not born, but created as issues of today develop into the conflicts of tomorrow. To quote Professor Conteh-Morgan who paraphrased Carl Van Clausewitz statement –

"Terrorism is nothing but the continuation of politics by other means".[179]

---

[179] Earl Conteh-Morgan, Collective Political Violence – An Introduction to the Theories and Cases of Violent Conflicts, Routledge, 2004, p258.

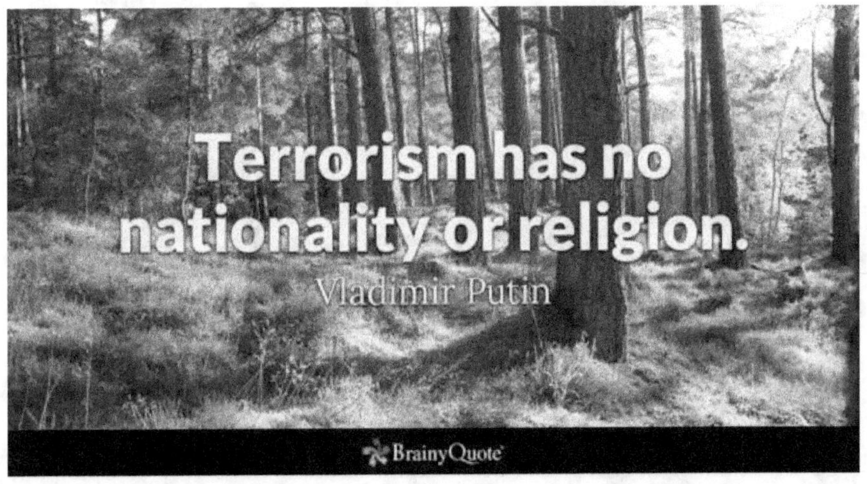

Terrorism has no nationality or religion. - Vladimir Putin[180]

U.S. soldiers stop traffic on the road to the governor's compound in Kandahar[181]

---

[180] https://www.brainyquote.com/topics/terrorism
[181] https://www.commondreams.org/news/2013/12/31/biggest-threat-world-peace-united-states

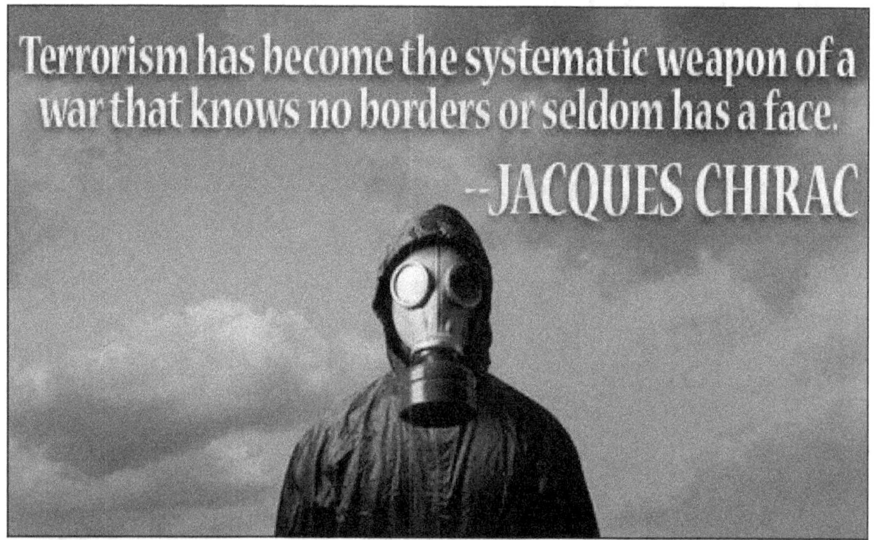
Terrorism has become the systematic weapon of a war that knows no borders or seldom has a face.
--JACQUES CHIRAC

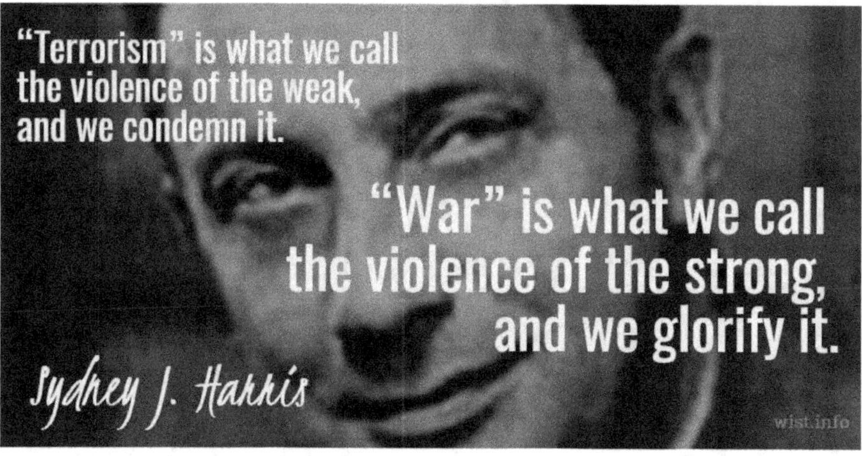
"Terrorism" is what we call
the violence of the weak,
and we condemn it.
"War" is what we call
the violence of the strong,
and we glorify it.
Sydney J. Harris
wist.info

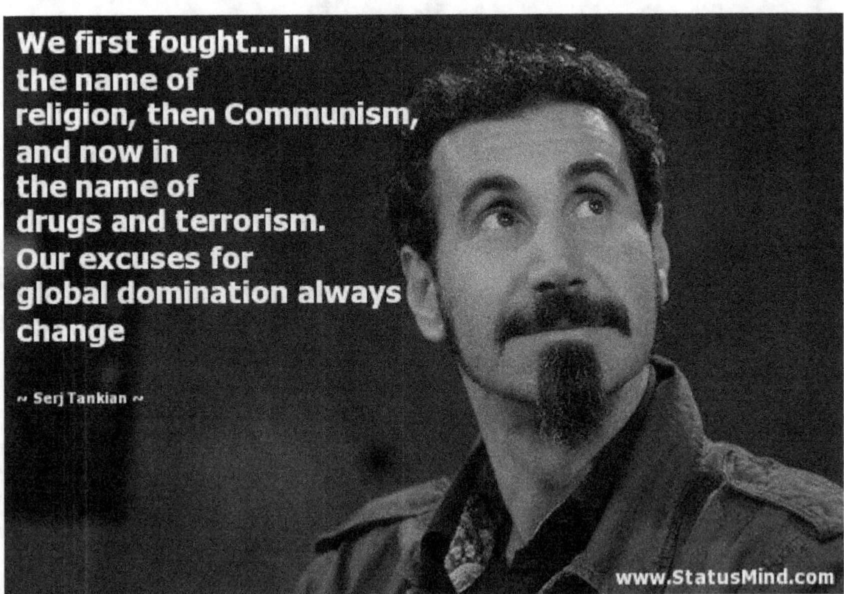
We first fought... in
the name of
religion, then Communism,
and now in
the name of
drugs and terrorism.
Our excuses for
global domination always
change
~ Serj Tankian ~
www.StatusMind.com

How can you have a war on
TERRORISM
when war itself is terrorism?
Howard Zinn on Terrorism via Gecko&Fly

With guns you can kill terrorists, with education you can kill terrorism.
Malala Yousafzai

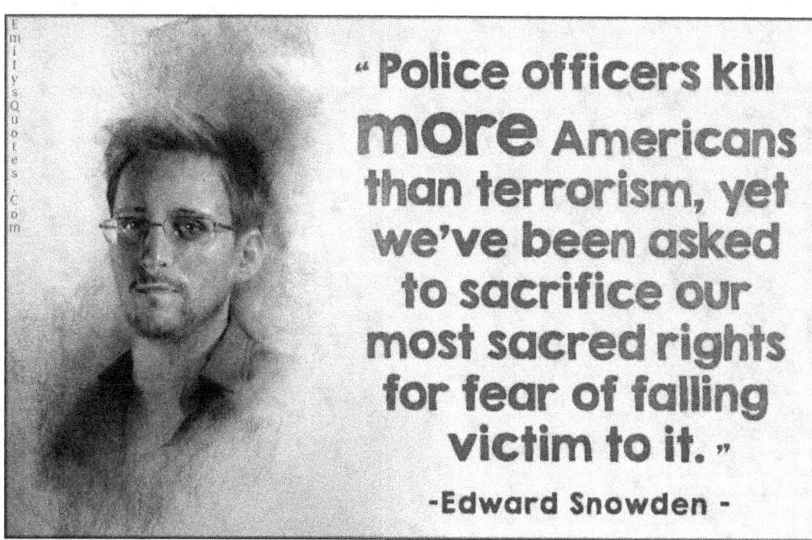
" Police officers kill more Americans than terrorism, yet we've been asked to sacrifice our most sacred rights for fear of falling victim to it. "
-Edward Snowden -

Terrorism has no religion, terrorists have no religion and they are friends of no religion,.

— Manmohan Singh

meetville.com

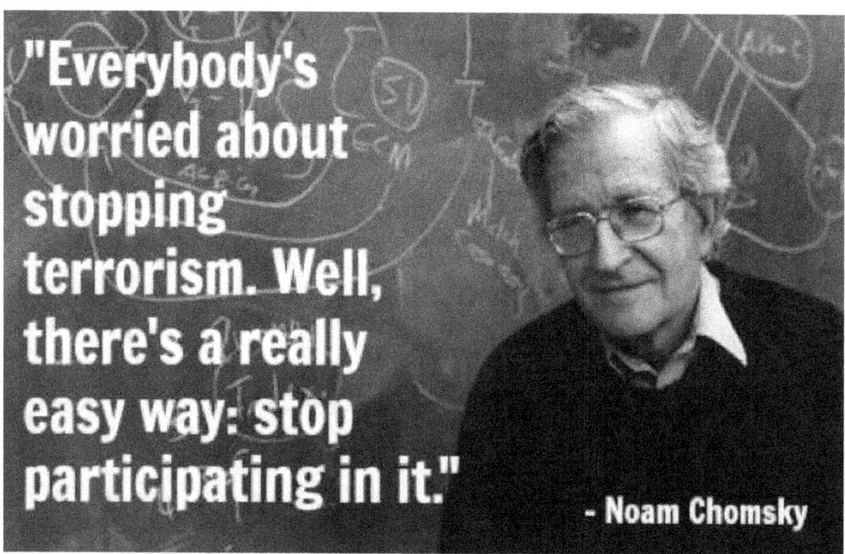
"Everybody's worried about stopping terrorism. Well, there's a really easy way: stop participating in it."
- Noam Chomsky

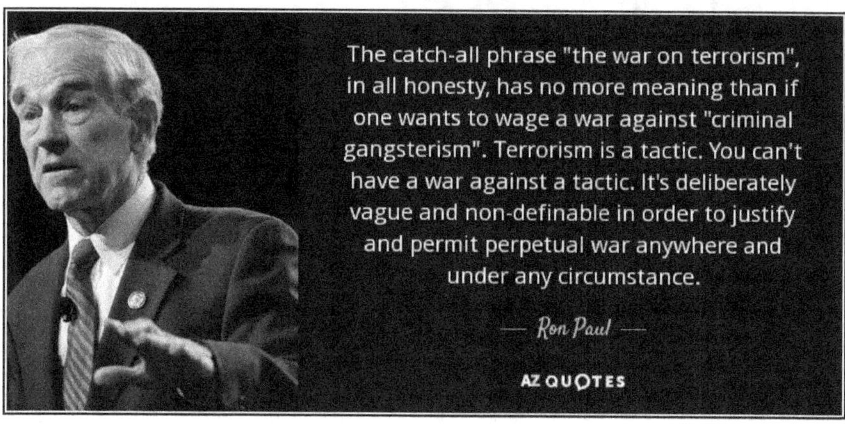
The catch-all phrase "the war on terrorism", in all honesty, has no more meaning than if one wants to wage a war against "criminal gangsterism". Terrorism is a tactic. You can't have a war against a tactic. It's deliberately vague and non-definable in order to justify and permit perpetual war anywhere and under any circumstance.
— Ron Paul —
AZ QUOTES

References

Adrian Guelke, (1998). The Age of Terrorism and the International Political System, I.B Tauris Publishers & Co Ltd.

Alan Collins, (2007). Contemporary Security Studies, Oxford University Press.

Amnesty International - https://www.amnesty.org.uk/

Bekerman, Z., & Zembylas, M. (2014). Some reflections on the links between teacher education and peace education: Interrogating the ontology of normative epistemological premises. Teaching and Teacher Education, 41, 52-59. doi:10.1016/j.tate.2014.03.002

Butt, M. N., Iqbal, M., Ud-Din, M. N., Hussain, I., & Muhammad, N. (2011). Infuse concept of peace in curriculum development. Contemporary Issues in Education Research (CIER), 4(2), 27. doi:10.19030/cier.v4i2.4080

Campaign Against Arms Trade (CAAT), Global Poverty, Online - https://www.caat.org.uk/issues/poverty

Cordesman, A.H. (1988). Armed Forces Journal, Western Strategic Interests and the India-Pakistan military balance, Ian Allan Ltd.

Culp, J. (2017). Against all odds: Peace education in times of crisis. Educational Philosophy and Theory, 49(10), 1029-1037. doi:10.1080/00131857.2016.1274954

Danesh, H. B. (2006). Towards an integrative theory of peace education. Journal of Peace Education, 3(1), 55-78. doi:10.1080/17400200500532151 Docklands Bombing (Internet Website - Wikipedia, the free encyclopedia) http://en.wikipedia.org/wiki/1996_Docklands_bombing

Earl Conteh-Morgan, Collective Political Violence – An Introduction to the Theories and Cases of Violent Conflicts, Routledge, 2004.

Frank Barnaby, Instruments of Terror, Vision Paperbacks, 1996.

French Revolution (Online)
http://en.wikipedia.org/wiki/French_revolution#Reign_of_Terror

Galtung, J. (1983). Peace education: Learning to hate war, love peace, and to do something about it. International Review of Education / Internationale Zeitschrift Für Erziehungswissenschaft / Revue Internationale De l'Education, 29(3), 281-287. doi:10.1007/BF00597972

Global Issues - http://www.globalissues.org/article/78/small-arms-they-cause-90-of-civilian-casualties

Gross, Z. (2017). Revisiting peace education: Bridging theory and practice – international and comparative perspectives – introduction. Research in Comparative and International Education, 12(1), 3-8. doi:10.1177/1745499917698290

Harris, I. M. (2004). Peace education theory. Journal of Peace Education, 1(1), 5-20. doi:10.1080/1740020032000178276

Hiroshima (Online) http://en.wikipedia.org/wiki/Hiroshima

Human Rights Watch (HRW) - https://www.hrw.org/news/2009/03/25/israel-white-phosphorus-use-evidence-war-crimes

James Adams, (1988). The Financing of Terror, New English Library.

Kit O'Connell (2016). Four Million Muslims Killed In Western Wars: Should We Call It Genocide? https://www.globalresearch.ca/four-million-muslims-killed-in-western-wars-should-we-call-it-genocide/5541926

Lauritzen, S. M. (2016). Building peace through education in a post-conflict environment: A case study exploring perceptions of best practices. International Journal of Educational Development, 51, 77-83. doi:10.1016/j.ijedudev.2016.09.001

Lawrence Freedman, (2002). Super terrorism Policy Responses, Blackwell Publishing, Ltd.

Lawrence Freedman, Christopher Hill, Adam Roberts, R.J. Vincent, Paul Wilkinson and Philip Windsor, (1986). Terrorism and International Order, Routledge & Keegan Paul Ltd.

Madrid Train Bombings (Online) http://en.wikipedia.org/wiki/Madrid_train_bombings

Moscow theater hostage (Online)

http://en.wikipedia.org/wiki/Moscow_theater_hostage_crisis

Munich Massacre (Online) http://en.wikipedia.org/wiki/Munich_massacre

Nafeez Ahmed (2017). Unworthy Victims: Western Wars Have Killed Four Million Muslims Since 1990 - http://www.stopwar.org.uk/index.php/news-comment/2615-unworthy-victims-western-wars-have-killed-four-million-muslims-since-1990

Oxfam - https://www.oxfam.org/en/research/wealth-having-it-all-and-wanting-more

Peter Hough, (2001). Understanding Global Security, Routledge.

Peter Sederberg, (1989). Terrorist: Myths, Illusion, Rhetoric and Reality, London; Prentice Hall.

Rainbow Warrior (Online) http://en.wikipedia.org/wiki/Sinking_of_the_Rainbow_Warrior

Rhodesian War (Online) http://en.wikipedia.org/wiki/Rhodesian_War

SIPRI - https://www.sipri.org/

Smith Ellison, C. (2014). The role of education in peacebuilding: An analysis of five change theories in sierra leone. Compare: A Journal of Comparative and International Education, 44(2), 186-207. doi:10.1080/03057925.2012.734138

Stavrianakis, A. (2010;2013;). Taking aim at the arms trade: NGOs, global civil society and the world military order. London;New York;: Zed Books. Stephenson, C. M. (2012). Elise boulding and peace education: Theory, practice, and quaker faith. Journal of Peace Education, 9(2), 115-126. doi:10.1080/17400201.2012.700196

Stop the War Coalition - http://www.stopwar.org.uk/index.php

Strategic Bombing (Online) http://en.wikipedia.org/wiki/Strategic_bombing_during_World_War_II

Terrorism theirs and ours (Online) – by Eqbal Ahmed http://www.sangam.org/ANALYSIS/Ahmad.htm

Terrorism, (2007). (Online) www. http://en.wikipedia.org/wiki/Terrorism

Terrorist incidents (Online)
http://en.wikipedia.org/wiki/List_of_terrorist_incidents

Walter Laqueur, (1999). The New Terrorism: Fanaticism and the Arms of Mass Destruction, Oxford.

Ward, V. (2009). Conflicts of interest: Plasticity of peace tourism and the 21st century nation. Perspectives on Global Development and Technology, 8(2-3), 414-426. doi:10.1163/156914909X423953

Wessells, M. (2005). Child soldiers, peace education, and postconflict reconstruction for peace. Theory into Practice, 44(4), 363-369. doi:10.1207/s15430421tip4404_10

WHO. (2017, September 15). World hunger again on the rise, driven by conflict and climate change, new UN report says. Retrieved July 19, 2018, from http://www.who.int/news-room/detail/15-09-2017-world-hunger-again-on-the-rise-driven-by-conflict-and-climate-change-new-un-report-says

William Crotty, (2005). Democratic development and Political Terrorism – The Global Perspective, Northeastern University Press.

Index

<u>Recently released books (2018)</u>

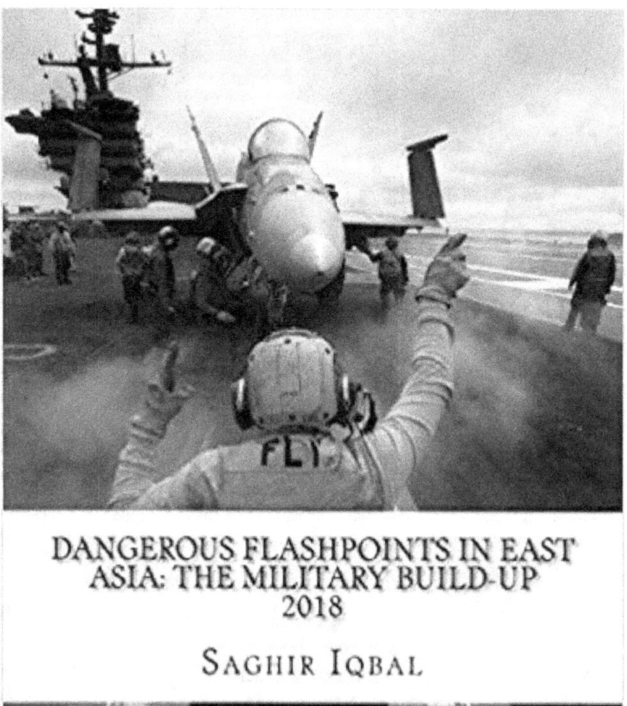

Major changes in East Asia have placed the region near the top of the World's strategic agenda. East Asia has until recently experienced the fastest regional economic growth rate in the world for many years. Economic co-operation has been flourishing and economic interests have become the major reason in reshaping East Asian international relations. However, there have also been changes in the security environment, due to many factors, such as the reduction of US forces in East Asia, the disintegration of the Soviet Union (the decline of the Soviet Union's presence in the region had led to renewed attention to traditional and potential rivalries among the major East Asian powers), and the concern of China's hegemonistic ambitions.

The astronomical rising costs of modern combat has resulted in many countries being deprived of purchasing a modern combat aircraft and this has had an adverse effect on their security. Many nations have tried to undertake cost-effective measures for their defence needs.

Countries can either purchase very expensive modern aircraft or buy older aircraft that can be expensive to operate due to their high maintenance requirements. The Pakistan Air Force had initiated the plan to co-develop an affordable modern multi-role fighter aircraft with China. Chengdu Aircraft Corporation (CAC) in collaboration with Pakistan Aeronautical Complex (PAC, Kamra) have jointly developed the JF-17 Thunder combat aircraft (also known as the FC-1 Xiaolong Fierce Dragon in China).

JF-17 Thunder is a sophisticated light-weight multi-role, all weather, day/night fighter aircraft that is manufactured by Pakistan and China. The JF-17 Thunder has become a very cost-effective aircraft that costs very little compared to other modern aircraft. Many countries have shown an interest and a few have started to make orders. Some have described the JF-17 as the 'Ultimate MiG-21' arguing that the Chinese/Pakistani JF-17 builds on a classic warplane – although it has no resemblance and its level of sophistication is comparable to current advanced fighter aircraft on the market. This very modern and capable aircraft has the potential to become a potent platform that can serve with numerous air forces across the world.

The global security challenges after the post-Cold war period has affected many countries. Pakistan's geography and location present its security planners with serious, almost irresolvable strategic and tactical problems. It borders the nuclear states of India and China, an ambitious Iran, and an unstable Afghanistan, which is perceived as a gateway to its commercial-strategic ambitions in Central Asia.

Pakistan's key security problems are a reflection of its history and domestic circumstances. The overriding concern of Pakistan is its internal and external security. Strategically, Pakistan lacks territorial depth. Its main cities and communication routes are relatively close to the border with India and are susceptible to attack. In addition, the headwaters of Pakistan's rivers and main irrigation systems originate from India. Pakistan's borders with India were also new and mainly unfortified and, in many places, were drawn in ways that made them indefensible. Because the borders were also un-demarcated, there was abundant chance for conflict. Pakistan has particularly been affected with a number of issues.

It has been argued by many that a Fourth generation/Hybrid war has been imposed on Pakistan, in order to break the nation (Balkanization of Pakistan into different parts) with the aim of making it either extremely weak or total destruction as a nation state (so that it is not able to challenge the hegemonistic ambitions of its adversaries).The purpose of this book is to assess the military security problems that Pakistan faces, and focus on its external security matters (military threats from neighbouring countries such as India, balance of power in the region, nuclear and ballistic missile threats, relationship with external powers, the high risk of war and its role on the 'War on Terror'), and its internal security problems (sectarianism, proliferation of small arms, refugees, ethnic violence, drug problem, economic weaknesses), and also its ability to cope with these problems.

MISCALCULATION: RISKS OF INADVERTENT NUCLEAR WAR

SAGHIR IQBAL

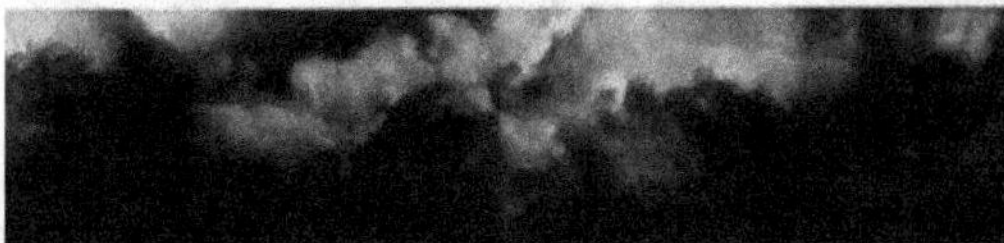

An impending nuclear holocaust is likely to happen, if the world community does not take action. A conflict that has been simmering for many years is beginning to spiral out of control. Two nuclear powers have an unresolved dispute that has increased tensions in the region.

Both countries are purchasing and developing sophisticated state-of-the-art weapons that could unleash great terror and destruction on the populations of both countries – with also serious global ramifications.

The world's most dangerous flashpoint, has the highest chance of a nuclear war occurring – it is deemed by many to be more serious that the Cuban Missile Crisis and North Korea's nuclear sabre rattling. The dispute needs to be amicably resolved between both nations and confidence building measures need to be implemented.

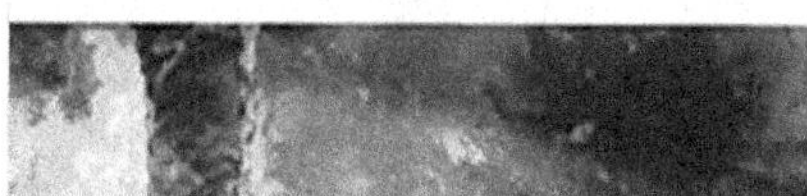

Pakistan faces a number of threats from internal and external forces – with the aim of weakening the country and an attempt to 'balkanise' Pakistan in to different parts. The Pakistani Chief of Army, General Qamar Javed Bajwa has said that "a hybrid war had been imposed on Pakistan to internally weaken it, but noted that the enemies were failing to divide the country on the basis of ethnicity and other identities".

Furthermore he states, "Our enemies know that they cannot beat us fair and square and have thus subjected us to a cruel, evil and protracted hybrid war. They are trying to weaken our resolve by weakening us from within". Conflicts in Ukraine, Israel and Lebanon (Hizbullah), Syria, Libya, War on Terror in Afghanistan and its impact in Pakistan etc., have resulted in multi-layered efforts to destabilise a functioning state and polarize its society. The centre of gravity is to target population in hybrid warfare. The aim of the adversary is to influence influential policy makers and key decision makers by combining kinetic operations with subversive efforts. The aggressor often resorts to covert actions, to avoid attribution or retribution. At the moment there is no universally accepted definition of hybrid wars – the term is too abstract and is seen by some as using a fancy term to refer to irregular methods to counter conventionally stronger forces.

Accordingly, many say that the new definitions of 4th generation or hybrid wars are really the repackaging of the traditional clash between the armed forces of nation states and the non-state insurgents. This book will be assessing Pakistan's insecurity and the hybrid wars imposed onto it by its adversaries. It will look at a number of issues that Pakistan is facing (military imbalance, economic and political weaknesses, internal and external security threats and the impact of hybrid warfare on Pakistan).

Each year billions of dollars' worth of arms are procured between various nations, despite the fact that many millions of people live in desperate poverty, many will die from hunger and hunger related diseases. Weapons of increasing firepower and the missiles to deliver them accurately are being acquired, mainly through the Global Arms Trade. This means that we must expect wars in the world to become increasingly violent and destructive.

This book focuses on what the arms trade is and its impact on the world, the wars which have resulted or were sustained by this trade. It is necessary to know which countries sell arms and which ones buy. Also it is important to have some idea of how large the trade is. The international trade in arms has considerably increased since World War 2. Major weapons (aircraft, missiles, tanks and ships) probably account for about one-half of the total trade in weapons and equipment. Many countries and their respective Military-Industrial Complex are 'making a killing' in the world's largest trade in the buying and selling of military technology (weapons).

The global security challenges since World War II and thereafter (post-Cold war period) has affected many countries. This has resulted in a number of countries pursuing a nuclear weapons programme to provide them with the ultimate security – the belief that the fear of utter annihilation of their opponents would result in deterrence and eventually detente. According to Kristensen and Norris (2014), there are approximately 16,300 nuclear weapons located at some 97 sites in 14 countries. Many of these weapons are in military arsenals (roughly 10,000), with the remaining ones being in the process of retirement and awaiting dismantlement. Accordingly, 93% of the total global inventory resides in Russia and the United States of America. The remaining weapon stockpiles are in the United Kingdom (UK), France, China, India, Pakistan, North Korea and Israel.

This book looks at the proliferation of weapons of mass destruction (WMD), the double standards and hypocrisy practiced by the five declared nuclear powers. It gives a brief short history of nuclear development in the nuclear countries and the impact of nuclear war. It argues that the only way to eradicate these horrendous weapons is for the five declared nuclear powers to make immediate measures to dismantle the weapons and stockpiles of weaponised materials – as they had agreed under the Nuclear Non-proliferation Treaty (NPT).

ABOUT THE AUTHOR

Saghir Iqbal is a researcher in International Relations and Security Studies. He is an experienced Intelligence Analyst and has achieved a number of qualifications in this field. He is also a Lecturer in Business Management as well as an Examiner for A Level History and Business. Saghir Iqbal has a subject specialism in the following areas:

International Politics of the Cold War 1945-1991
Conflict Resolution in International Society+
Global and North-South Security Studies
Britain in the World
Disarmament Processes: History and Theory
Nationalism and Ethnicity in Post-Cold War Politics
Middle East: Area in Conflict
European Security
International Politics of the Environment
The United Nations, Peacekeeping and Intervention
Disarmament Processes: Current Problems
Globalisation and the South
International Terrorism
International Politics and Security Studies
Introduction to Peace Studies
Politics of the Global Environment
Regional Security in East Asia
Critical Security studies

Recently released books (2018)

- Dangerous Flashpoints in East Asia: The Military Build-up
- JF-17 Thunder: The Making of a Modern Cost- effective Multi-role Combat Aircraft
- Pakistan's War Machine: An Encyclopedia of its Weapons, Strategy and Military Security
- Miscalculation: Risks of Inadvertent Nuclear War
- Hybrid Warfare and its Impact on Pakistan's Security
- Making a Killing: The Scourge of the Global Arms Trade
- Nuclear Apartheid: Bullying, Hypocrisy and the Double Standards on Nuclear Weapons

Website: www.saghir.co.uk